PENGUIN ANANDA

# THE INNER JOURNEY

Vraja Bihari Das, also known as Venugopal Acharya, is a highly respected spiritual teacher and author of five books. He has been a full-time monk at Sri Sri Radha Gopinath Mandir, Mumbai, for two and a half decades. Despite his background in finance and corporate work, his true passion lies in teaching Vedic philosophy.

Vraja Bihari is a member of the temple care committee and congregation development department, where he provides counselling to young men in the monastery and trains a satellite community of over 100 families in various parts of Mumbai. He is renowned for his knowledge of Vedic texts and his ability to connect them to modern life. He offers lectures and seminars for students, professionals and anyone seeking emotional and spiritual fulfilment. Bhakti Yoga, a practice of devotional worship, is a core aspect of his teachings.

His website, www.yogaformodernage.com, contains over 1100 articles, and he also has a YouTube channel. His books include *Are You Connected?* and *Mind Your Mind*, which offer tools for better relationships and inner peace, as well as *Lessons from the Road*, which shares insights from Vedic scriptures.

As a seasoned international speaker, Vraja Bihari has given talks in the USA, Australia, the UK, Germany, Russia, and other parts of Europe and the Middle East. His candid thoughts on mental hygiene, spiritual discipline and finding deep emotional fulfilment resonate with people from all walks of life.

# THE INNER JOURNEY

## Finding a Safe Space amidst Chaos

## VRAJA BIHARI DAS

PENGUIN
ANANDA

An imprint of Penguin Random House

PENGUIN ANANDA

Penguin Ananda is an imprint of the Penguin Random House group of companies
whose addresses can be found at global.penguinrandomhouse.com

Published by Penguin Random House India Pvt. Ltd
4th Floor, Capital Tower 1, MG Road,
Gurugram 122 002, Haryana, India

Penguin
Random House
India

First published in Penguin Ananda by Penguin Random House India 2024

ISBN 9780143469261

Typeset in Adobe Caslon Pro by MAP Systems, Bengaluru, India
Printed at Replika Press Pvt. Ltd, India

www.penguin.co.in

*To Srila Prabhupada, who guided me and thousands of others on our inner journeys, and to my grandparents, who taught me the virtues of slowing down and living with grace*

# Contents

# Introduction

*That supreme abode of Mine is not illumined by the sun or*
*moon, nor by fire or electricity. Those who reach it never return*
*to this material world.*

—Bhagavad Gita (15.6)

Imagine being forced to enter a deadly, lonely forest all alone.
The eerie and foreboding darkness sends shivers down your
spine as wolves howl incessantly and the occasional roar of a
tiger pierces the silence. Given the choice, you would likely
run away from this jungle and seek the safety of your home.

In a similar way, our inner world of mind, intelligence
and ego can feel like a dark and dangerous jungle that scares
many of us. As our mind incessantly whines, we long to escape
to the safety of our homes, but we often don't know where our
home is or how to find it.

The purpose of this book is to facilitate our discovery of
our inner home and provide solace in its safe chambers.

We have two lives: one is the obvious external life, where
our social dealings and actions can be seen and judged by
others, and the other is our internal hopes and horrors, known
only to us. But do we truly know our inner selves? Do we face
our inner demons, do we avoid them or, even worse, suppress

our unhealthy desires? Many of us run away from what we imagine is a deadly forest within us. We bury ourselves in our smartphones, social media apps and countless web series instead of entering the treacherous woods of our own thoughts and feelings. We would do anything to avoid facing our own insecurities.

It's easy to live in denial of our dark side—our fears and undesirable anxieties are often unknown even to ourselves. Meanwhile, our life-alienating emotions gather energy within us, eventually taking a toll on our physical and emotional well-being. It's important to face our inner selves and come to terms with our inner demons if we want to lead a fulfilling life. The essays and reflections I share in this book aim to guide us in exploring the uncharted territory of our inner world and help us understand and accept ourselves better.

To truly understand ourselves, we must face both the joys and sorrows, the pleasant and unpalatable, which make up our inner world. It's then that we can enter our 'Heart Space', our home within.

After a long and tiring day, we all long to reach the comfort of our physical homes. Similarly, in our inner world, we need a place where we feel rested and safe. During the day, when different challenges confront our mind and ego, we yearn for a sense of belongingness and to be loved and accepted without judgement.

This sacred space is within our own hearts. While the physical heart is a muscular organ that pumps blood through our blood vessels, this book is not about that. Across various religions, cultures and traditions spanning millennia, the heart has been identified as the seat of emotion and life. It's a symbol of love that signifies truth, conscience and connection.

In this book, we explore this emotional and spiritual heart, which is our true home and a source of solace in the midst of life's relentless challenges.

Throughout this book, you will see the terms 'Heart Space' and 'Home State' used interchangeably. That's because, in our relationships and work in this world, we feel at home when our hearts are safe. Similarly, our homes are where our hearts are secure and we feel a sense of belongingness.

The two terms are synonymous and represent the idea that when we feel emotionally safe and secure, we are at home. It's when we have a deep sense of connection with ourselves and others that we experience well-being and happiness, and that's what we explore in this book.

Just as we have a physical home in the material world, we also have a home in our inner world. When our hearts beat with healthy emotions and a sense of 'all's well', we can experience inner peace even amidst external chaos. This safe space of our hearts is our real home in our internal world.

In this book, I delve into the practices and values that help develop a strong and vibrant heart, one that beats with joy and gratitude throughout the day.

This book aims to answer three key questions:

1. What is the Heart Space (or Home State)?
2. Why is it important to live in the Heart Space?
3. How do we live and flourish in our Heart Space?

While the first two questions will be addressed briefly, the main focus of this book is on the third question: discovering and thriving in our Home State. We will explore various strategies and techniques to help cultivate a sense of safety, peace and affiliation with our inner world. The third section has ten carefully chosen essays (from Chapters 7 to 16) that systematically take us on a journey from understanding the importance of slowing down our lives to chanting the Holy Names of God with love and feeling. It is the most important section in which I candidly share Bhakti Yoga practices and paradigms, as I have learnt as a monk for over twenty-five years in our little Mumbai monastery.

We will also delve into the topic of God. All traditions recognize a power beyond us—a benevolent divinity-like figure. Some cultures call this figure Almighty Father or God, while others refer to it as 'Brahman'. If you're a *Star Wars* fan, you may refer to it as 'The Force'. In the Harry Potter series, the characters swear by Merlin, the half-mythical, half-historical character, during trying times. In *The Lord of the Rings*, it's Gandalf the Grey, the angel incarnate, who guides the protagonists of *The Fellowship of the Ring* as well as the dwarves. He is there to protect Bilbo Baggins in *The Hobbit* as well. In the Terminator franchise, the antagonistic force is the artificial superintelligence system called Skynet, and it is John Connor who rallies human resistance against Skynet's machines. The victory of the resistance is achieved through sheer human will.

The battle between good and evil is therefore eternal. In the spiritual tradition I come from, we refer to the internal guide or 'the force' as *paramatma* or Krishna—the beautiful Supreme Personality of Godhead, who helps His devotees overcome all obstacles in their attempt to live in congruence with timeless devotional principles.

In this book, we will use the words God and Krishna synonymously, to help us connect with a force beyond us— the kind and compassionate Lord who guides all sincere seekers who wish to live in the Home State and helps others discover their Heart Space as well.

I have also added references and incidents from the life of His Divine Grace A.C. Bhaktivedanta Swami Srila Prabhupada, the founder *acharya* (teacher/guru) of the worldwide spiritual society called the International Society for Krishna Consciousness (or ISKCON for short). His wisdom has been a beacon for me during my twenty-five-year-long spiritual journey.

Interestingly, the more we connect with God, the less daunting the forest within us appears. We come to realize that it's a luxuriant landscape with verdant bushes, fragrant flowers and lush shade-giving trees with ripe fruits. The journey inwards can be a refreshing and fulfilling experience.

This book is a voyage to change our perspective—to see the forest within us for what it is—a beautiful Vrindavan forest where God, Krishna, resides eternally with His devotees, beckoning us to His world of love and happiness.

# Part I

# Chapter 1

# What Is the Heart Space
# (or a Home State)?

*For the self, there is neither birth nor death at any time. He has
not come into being, does not come into being and will not come
into being. He is unborn, eternal, ever-existing and primeval.
He is not slain when the body is slain.*

—Bhagavad Gita (2.20)

As I looked down at my fully drenched body, I realized with
disgust that the latrine water had found its way onto me,
mixing with the rainwater and leaving me feeling desperate to
get out. I was at a friend's place in a low-lying area, and as the
rain continued to pour, the drainage from all the houses in the
colony overflowed, filling the streets with neck-deep effluent.
It was a harrowing experience, and it wasn't until late evening
that my friend's family was finally safe at a shelter.

Meanwhile, I was still desperate to get to my own home,
but the rain showed no signs of stopping, and there were no
buses or taxis available. So, I trudged through the muddy
streets for hours, feeling sick and icky as the slops from the
street soaked into my skin.

3

Finally, at midnight, I arrived at my safe sanctuary—a well-maintained apartment in a decent locality in Mumbai. I ran to the shower and let the cooling water wash away the filth, staying there for a long time. Afterwards, I drank some hot soup and relaxed on the sixth-floor balcony overlooking the ocean. It was a relief to be home, to be in my 'Home State', where I knew I was safe and could feel a sense of belonging and shelter.

Just as we have a physical home that provides us shelter from external elements, we also need an inner Home State to provide us with a sense of security and peace amidst life's challenges. Whether it's unexpected setbacks, misunderstandings with loved ones or overwhelming emotions that leave us feeling drained and disconnected, we all need a refuge that we can turn to in times of need.

While Netflix or motivational videos can provide temporary relief, they often fail to address the root of our problems. In moments of true introspection, we realize that the void inside us cannot be filled by external sources alone. This is when we can begin to explore our spiritual side and find deeper meaning and purpose in our lives.

Rather than simply learning the techniques of meditation, we must delve into the essence of it, exploring the innermost recesses of our hearts and minds. By doing so, we can find a sense of belonging and connection that transcends the limitations of our physical reality, providing us with a lifelong source of comfort and support.

## Expanding the Heart

A troubled young man sought the guidance of a wise sage, expressing his anxieties and constant worries. In response, the elderly monk, dressed in bright saffron robes, asked the young man to get a palmful of salt and pour it into a cup of water. He then asked him to drink it, which made the young man puke. The sage then took the young man to a nearby lake and asked him to pour a handful of salt into the crystal-clear water. He then asked the young man to drink it, and this time the water tasted sweet.

The sage imparted his wisdom, saying, 'We all face the same set of worries and problems, which are like a handful of salt. The difference between us lies in our hearts. Is it small, like a cup of water or is it large and benevolent, like a beautiful lake? If you live with a scarcity mindset, always focusing on your inadequacies and fears, you are living in a constricted Heart Space. When problems, like the palmful of salt, enter your small heart cup, you'll feel overwhelmed with bitterness. The material world will continue to throw challenges at you, and you'll become internally disgusted with life. However, if you learn to expand your Heart Space and make it big and beautiful like a lake of sweet water, if you live with abundance and gratitude, then you'll be able to withstand the whirlwind that blows your way. The worries of this world won't affect you, and you'll taste the sweetness of life in your earthly journey.'

The choice is ours: are we willing to open our hearts to newer and exciting possibilities? Can we live in this expanded Heart Space, which is our real home in the inner world?

## Purifying Emotions: The 'Heart' of Meditation

An expanded Heart Space or Home State involves purifying our emotions and developing spiritual sentiments. Most spiritual traditions advocate meditation as a practice to make the mind peaceful. However, the school of Bhakti Yoga, which

ISKCON belongs to and where I have been a practicing monk for over twenty-five years, teaches the science of cultivating beautiful spiritual emotions for God.

For a Bhakti Yoga practitioner, meditation truly means expanding the mind and eventually going beyond it to enter the space of the heart.

Here's a simple meditation exercise you can try right now: Imagine if God appeared before you at this moment and asked you to thank Him for any three gifts you received in the last twenty-four hours.

Slow down your mind, take a deep breath and search for the answers. Perhaps being alive and healthy is something you're thankful for or maybe you had an exotic breakfast that you enjoyed, and the fact that you could relish it is a matter of celebration.

The first step is to think—search for an event to thank the Lord. Then, enter the space of that episode and feel the emotions of gratitude. Even if you can't thank God for many gifts, the fact that you are searching for a 'thank you' emotion makes you move from your head to the heart, and your heart expands. You'll notice that your heart is filled with a desire for gratitude. This is the 'heart of meditation'.

Problems and challenges are inevitable in our lives, such as struggling to find a new job, paying our mortgage or experiencing difficulties in a relationship. However, for a Bhakti Yoga practitioner, a daily practice of chanting the Holy Names of God or offering prayers of gratitude can help us transcend the mind and enter the space of the heart.

While it's common to analyse external events and people using our minds, it's also important to examine the state of our own mind. Instead of fully identifying with our thoughts, we can practise stepping back and cultivating awareness.

Through slow breathing and fostering positive emotions like gratitude, we can expand our Heart Space and live in our true Home in the inner world. We will then not only see the world through our mind; we'll also see our mind!

In essence, meditation involves living in the space of the Heart, where, with more awareness and gratitude, we enter the world of the real 'I'—the soul. This is an emotional–spiritual realm that nourishes and energizes us.

## A New Perspective on Meditation

Many meditation teachers present meditation as a tool to control the mind. The focus is often on bringing the mind back to one's breath, the sound of a mantra or the tip of one's nose. However, here we explore a new perspective on meditation.

Drawing from the ancient Indian text, the *Taittiriya Upanishad* (2.1-5), which explains the different sheaths that cover our real selves, we delve into the subtlest of all coverings on our consciousness: the anandamaya kosha, or the bliss sheath.[1]

Our true self, known as *atma*, exists beyond the body, mind, intelligence and all our feelings. The fact that we can identify and explain our bodily sensations or our mental state, name our feelings and describe our thoughts, means that we—the 'real I', the self—are different from all these emotions. There is someone or something that experiences all these sensations and acknowledges that 'I was thinking hard' or 'I was in deep, dreamless sleep.' Who is that 'I'?

According to Vedic texts, the true self, atma, is enclosed by five sheaths, with the gross physical body being the outermost covering. The next layer is the vital life force, or breath, known as prana. The third layer is the mind and senses (manomaya), followed by the faculty of intellect and wisdom that exercises determination and introspection (vijnanamaya). The fifth and closest layer to the soul is the anandamaya or happiness sheath. This layer is characterized by eternity, consciousness and bliss, known as *satcitananda*. Developing this sheath can lead to deep contentment, and regardless of how bad our external circumstances are, we can experience happiness if this sheath is developed.

When an emotional state or an activity of meditation helps us access this deep, inner self, we are living in the Heart Space—our real home in the inner world. It's in this space that we feel totally sheltered and are situated in our true glory or we are in a state that is known as satcitananda—eternity, consciousness and bliss.

When we talk of Heart Space or Home State, we are referring to that state of being in our internal life that is totally anchored and sheltered—a sense of belongingness engulfs the person; they are safe, loved and one with the universe.

## Three Houses in Our Inner World

A friend of mine who owns homes in Zurich, Los Angeles and Mumbai once told me that his 'real' home was in Mumbai, where he felt a sense of shelter and belonging. In the same manner, in our inner world also, we could reside at any one of the below three places at any given time:

1. The house of pleasure, where we indulge in fantasies and illusions that gratify our senses.
2. The house of problem solving, where we analyse and strategize to overcome challenges and achieve our goals.

3.  The Home State/Heart Space, the abode of surrender, shelter and peaceful experiences, where we feel a sense of belongingness and safety.

For instance, during a business meeting at the office, our physical body may be present, but our mind may wander off into a pleasurable fantasy or focus on problem-solving tasks, such as making a grocery list or comparing housing schemes. You may be engrossed in planning the next big project or you could be simmering with anger towards your neighbour for carelessly discarding their garbage on your lawn. When your mind is occupied with battling various challenges, you are residing in the house of struggle.

Alternatively, you could be fully engaged in the present moment, detached from any sense of control or fear. You are free from worry or the need for approval and you are fully aware of the time and your surroundings. You are at peace with yourself and with what is happening at the moment. This is the place where you reside in the house of peace. You may be spontaneously offering a silent prayer to your loving Lord or simply breathing deeply, surrendering to the universe. This is when you are in your Home State—your Heart Space. At this point, you have tapped into Anandamaya kosha—the bliss sheath—which is the closest to your real identity, the soul.

By recognizing these three inner abodes, we can consciously choose to enter the Home State/Heart Space, where we feel truly anchored and sheltered in our inner world.

The ability to take charge of one's inner world through mindfulness and absorption in social situations separates successful individuals from mediocre ones. The same holds true for top tennis players; their skills, practice and match experiences are similar. The key factor that distinguishes champions from the almost-best is their mental toughness, their ability to handle pressure and stay focused during critical moments.

To achieve success, it's crucial to be aware of where the mind is dwelling—whether it's absorbed in daydreaming and pleasure-seeking (sense gratification), planning solutions to problems (struggle) or simply experiencing peace and surrender (shelter). These are the three houses of our inner world where we can dwell at any given moment.

While the struggle to survive and the pursuit of pleasure seem natural, we as humans have the potential to rise beyond these states and spend at least some time daily in a place of surrender. By practising surrender, we can eventually live our whole day in this state, transcending the struggle and pleasure-seeking that so often consume us.

## Daily Case Studies of Living in the Three Internal Houses

My personal experiences and observations in the monastery may illustrate the principle of three houses and Home State better:

### Sense Gratification (Pleasure Seeker)

I sat in a meditative pose, while enjoying samosas and jalebis in my mind.

I was famished and had already been awake since 3 a.m., with three more hours to go before breakfast. As I silently fingered my prayer beads, I turned to my monk friend in charge of the kitchen and casually asked what would be served for breakfast. He was clearly annoyed and responded with a straight face, 'Hot samosas and jalebis.' Not realizing he was being sarcastic, I internally celebrated and reassured myself that enduring the next three hours of meditation in the temple would be worth it for the delicious feast to come.

As I sat with my fellow monks for our morning meditation, thoughts of delicious Indian snacks danced in my mind. I imagined myself biting into a crispy samosa filled with exotic flavours and spreading some tomato chutney on top. Jalebi, a crispy sweet treat from my childhood, was also on my mind.

Despite my indulgent daydreams, I remained dedicated to my meditation practice, sitting with my eyes closed, focusing on my breath and chanting. However, I couldn't resist the smile that kept creeping onto my face as I thought about the tasty treats waiting for me.

After the meditation session ended, a senior community member approached me and expressed his admiration for my dedication and focus during the chanting. He praised me for being an inspiration to others and thanked me for my commitment to spiritual practice.

Although I appreciated his kind words, I couldn't help but chuckle to myself as I realized that my mind had been consumed with thoughts of food rather than spiritual enlightenment. I didn't have the heart to disappoint him by sharing my true thoughts, so I graciously accepted his praise and left the scene.

While my body was present in the temple, my mind had been transported to the world of sensory pleasures. Despite this small diversion, I remained committed to my spiritual path and felt grateful for the simple joys of life, such as the anticipation of a delicious meal.

## Struggle (Problem Solver)

One of my monk friends, who is loved by all but has a shy nature, was asked to participate in one of our monastery's annual drama performances. Each year, the community eagerly anticipates the drama festival, which includes four to five professional performances as well as a play put on by our monastery. Despite his initial reluctance, my friend eventually agreed to a cameo role as a soldier who delivers just two lines in the hour-long production: 'Who is Yamuna? The king has sent a palanquin for you.'

During rehearsals, we quickly realized why our friend was hesitant to act. He was nervous and struggled with his dialogue, but he persisted in practising until he finally got it right on the final rehearsal. He had practised speaking the dialogue for four hours!

On the day of the performance, we all attended our regular spiritual programmes and Japa meditation sessions. About forty-five minutes into the session, while everyone was quietly chanting and meditating, a loud voice suddenly boomed through the temple hall, interrupting our peace: 'Who is Yamuna? The king has sent a palanquin for you!' We were all stunned and looked in the direction of the sound, only to find that our shy friend had unknowingly blurted out his dialogue at full volume. Although we couldn't help but laugh at his unintended outburst, he was understandably embarrassed.

While we were physically present in the sacred temple space, our friend was mentally immersed in his internal struggle to perfect his dialogue delivery. He was determined to solve this problem and was so absorbed in his own world that his performance manifested in the external world, much to his embarrassment.

Despite the unexpected disruption to our meditation session, we were all grateful for the humour and lightness our friend brought to the situation. We knew that, in his own way, he was fully committed to his role in the play and had put in the effort to overcome his shyness and deliver his lines with confidence.

## Shelter (Peace Experiencer)

My driver had been awake for the past fifty-five hours, and unfortunately, I was trapped in the vehicle with him. We were on a tour of villages in eastern India and had set off towards the holy city of Puri, in Odisha, before dawn. I asked him why he hadn't rested in the past two days, and he admitted that he had been busy arranging and concluding various programmes for my whirlwind tour.

As he swerved and turned on the narrow roads, I grew anxious. Driving through the remote areas of Odisha, he tried to reassure me that he was experienced and would get us to our destination safely. Though he was driving, I sat beside him and imagined that I was in control of the vehicle. While outwardly chanting my prayers on the beads, inwardly, I was struggling—navigating the vehicle through the rough terrain in the wee hours of the morning.

I kept engaging the driver in conversation to keep him awake and regularly checked on him to reassure myself that I was secure. In reality, however, I was completely helpless and dependent on him. After an hour of this harrowing ordeal, I realized that it had drained me of all my energy and my Japa session had become a distracted performance. I desperately needed to let go and enter the surrender zone.

I finally took a leap of faith and told the driver to wake me only when we arrived in Puri. I closed my eyes and focused on my chanting, despite my mind's wild wanderings and fears as the car navigated sharp turns. Despite my urges to look at the driver or seek reassurance, I kept returning to my mantra and breathing deeply. Gradually, my mind relaxed and I entered a state of peace and surrender. Time passed unnoticed and when the driver finally called out to me as we approached the outskirts of Puri, I felt a profound sense of joy and belonging. Even before arriving at the holy land of Jagannath Puri, I had already found a sense of home within myself.

## Let Go of the Struggle

The defining quality of a Home State is the ability to let go of the struggle.

Once, a king held a painting competition and two portraits made it to the final round. The first painting depicted a serene countryside with a beautiful sunrise and a bird cheerfully chirping on a branch of a banyan tree. The painting evoked a sense of tranquillity in the viewers' hearts. The second painting showed a cyclone with trees blown away by powerful winds and rivers flooding their banks. As thunderstorms hit the fields, a crow sat peacefully and noiselessly on a branch, drenched in the incessant showers.

To everyone's surprise, the king declared the second painting the winner of the contest. When asked to explain his decision, he said that the second painting presented a more accurate representation of reality. Life is tough, and we are constantly amidst one crisis or another. The restful crow teaches us to find peace within, even as the world outside of us crumbles and resurrects. The unwavering connection to a reality beyond this world is the space of surrender, even as persistent cyclones attack our inner world. Thus, the second painting better captures the essence of a Home State—the ability to find peace and surrender to a reality beyond ourselves, even amidst the most challenging situations.

As we age, some people tend to become more irritable and angry, unable to let go of things that bother them. Others may tolerate situations externally, but internally they seethe with pain. However, there are a few who thrive in the space of surrender, welcoming change and embracing new situations with gratitude.

I once met an eighty-five-year-old relative who sat peacefully while his family organized a day-long prayer festivity for his good health and happiness. As different family members and friends showered love and sought his blessings, he was the quintessence of grace. When I asked him how he was feeling that day, he calmly replied, 'I feel grateful. I agreed to participate in this prayer programme because this is how I can express my gratitude to the good Lord above for all that He has blessed me with over the last eighty-five years.' He then recounted all his blessings, and I was deeply inspired because I had known him personally for over four decades and seen that his life hadn't been entirely smooth; yet he chose to live in the present with gratitude. He had surrendered to what was happening in his life.

During the annual pilgrimage of our community to Vrindavan, I had the good fortune of interviewing Usha Mataji, a ninety-four-year-old woman who had the exuberance of a young girl. She was the first to rush to the classes and happily participated in *kirtans* (chanting) and visits to holy temples. While many of the younger members showed fatigue, she was the first to reach the venue for any event. I complimented Usha

Mataji on her cheerful and unassuming nature, and she smiled graciously. I then asked her if she had experienced many ups and downs in her life, to which she replied instantly, 'What can be more painful for a mother than seeing her own children die before her own eyes? I have lost three of my children to old age, but I have accepted the pain and moved on with gratitude.'

The first sign of surrender is to accept the unchangeable and then focus on your purpose. Srila Prabhupada, the founder acharya of the worldwide society of Krishna consciousness, also known as ISKCON, exemplified this on many occasions.

Once, while flying from Dallas to New Orleans, Srila Prabhupada's plane encountered rough weather. The plane swerved and lurched violently, tossed by the stormy air currents, and the overhead bins snapped open, causing articles to fall out. Passengers screamed in fear and confusion. Srila Prabhupada inquired about the situation and, upon learning about the stormy weather, remained calm. He sat quietly, chanting on his prayer beads, while his accompanying assistant, Upendra, worried and then reassured himself that it was all right if death were to come now, as he was with his spiritual master. Srila Prabhupada, however, showed no emotions—his eyes closed in prayer, and he was absorbed in his thoughts. Later, when the plane landed safely, passengers cheered loudly, but Srila Prabhupada remained grave and in equipoise. Upendra wondered what his spiritual master thought and hoped to get a purport to the incident. As they disembarked the plane, Srila Prabhupada finally spoke, and Upendra eagerly listened. 'How far is the temple from the airport?' Srila Prabhupada asked nonchalantly, and there was nothing else to discuss.

When we learn to live in the Heart Space for some time every day, it becomes a habit. Thus, when a tragedy or crisis strikes, we seamlessly gravitate to this state, finding acceptance and peace naturally.

During the devastating Indian Ocean tsunami that rocked over fourteen countries, including coastal Sri Lanka, in December 2004, claiming over 2,25,000 lives, ISKCON devotees rushed to provide aid. Among them was Indradyumna Swami and his team, who travelled to Sri Lanka as part of the relief efforts. The army chief overseeing the operations asked the devotees if they could offer something to help restore the spirits of the people affected by the disaster. The chief explained that while relief and food supplies had arrived quickly and there was no shortage of medical support, what was lacking was emotional balance—the psyche of the people had taken a heavy toll. The devotees responded with prayerful chanting, dancing, kirtans and community prayers, as well as distributing hot, vegetarian, sanctified food. Everywhere they went, people flocked to them and begged them to stay longer. The healing power of the Lord's Holy Names had transformed the hearts of the devastated people and provided a sense of shelter. The palpable peace that the villagers experienced was the desperate need of the hour, and the significance of living in a Home State was realized in such extraordinary situations.

## Three Stages of Our Lives

Imagine a man riding in a chariot with five horses dragging the miserable passenger in all directions, against his will. A soul trapped in this world of enjoyment and suffering is like riding the chariot of his life dragged by his mind and senses. That's the first stage.

In the second stage, he decides to hold the reins of the horses and manoeuvre the chariot as he wills. After a while, he realizes that the horses are wild and his attempts to control the chariot are feeble.

He then chooses the third phase—spiritual life, where he allows God to take charge of the chariot. He lets go of the reins.

The difference between the first and third stage is that in the first stage, when he lets go, it was his mind that dragged the chariot of his life, but now when he releases control, it's God who has taken charge. The difference in these two approaches is the inner aspiration: his desire has changed from wanting to be an enjoyer in this world to wanting to be a servant of God and His devotees. Until the soul makes this conscious choice to be a servant, he is relentlessly pummelled by the indefatigable material energy. We all surrender—either to the mind or to God. In between, we show our sincerity by struggling to control the mind. As we realize the formidable challenge ahead of us, we humbly call out to God, in deep realization of our puny existence and His magnificent omnipotence.

| STAGE 1 Pleasure Seeker | STAGE 2 Problem Solver | STAGE 3 Peace Experiencer |
|---|---|---|
| Body and senses | Mind–Intelligence–Ego | Heart and Soul (Home State/ Heart Space) |
| Sense gratification | Struggle | Surrender/Shelter |

## Reflections from a Case Study from
### *Śrīmad-Bhāgavatam*

*The crocodile's invincible jaws have got me. But the bigger tragedy is that I am unaware of its vicious grip, even though its terrible gaping maw inflicts continuous pain, with brief moments of relief that I take as pleasure. In times of mental clarity, I realize I can't get out of this deadly trap unless I call out to the Lord in utter surrender.*

—My journal reflections

Thousands of years ago, in a higher world, an elephant king named Gajendra was captured by a crocodile in a lake. The elephant was sporting with his many wives when, unexpectedly, a crocodile grabbed his leg in its jaws. Gajendra tried to escape, but water is home to aquatic predators, and for the elephant king, it was a foreign environment. He struggled, and even his wives and children tried pulling him away. But the crocodile just wouldn't let go. Exasperated, Gajendra's family left him to navigate the crisis alone.

This incident is narrated in *Śrīmad-Bhāgavatam*, a scripture that describes life, the world and relationships from a dimension different from the reality we commonly perceive with our limited senses. The explanations of the cosmos by modern science and *Śrīmad-Bhāgavatam* vary because they view the universe from different scales of perception. For example, I may see a grey powder, but you may view it under a microscope and discover that it's white and black granules. What exactly is it? Although the two views differ, each is correct according to perspective. We will study the spiritual significance of *Śrīmad-Bhāgavatam* in greater detail later in Section 3, Chapter 14, entitled, 'Three sacred principles of Prayer'.

*Śrīmad-Bhāgavatam* describes the universe from a scale of observation different from that of modern science, and in its stated purpose and scheme of things, there are special planets with extraordinary creatures and animals. For example, the animals talk and pray, and they experience life differently than animals do here on earth. Yet even in the twenty-first century, the principles that emerge from their stories, including Gajendra's struggle, which lasted for centuries, have a universal appeal and deliver lessons to a spiritual aspirant.

In his pain and suffering, Gajendra realized he needed to take his existence to the next level—to that of surrender. He called out to God helplessly and promised he'd offer his entire existence only to serve and please the Lord. He realized that no one could help him in this moment of crisis and that he was all alone in this dangerous world of suffering. The moment his appeal was sincere and heartfelt, the Lord descended on Garuda, His giant eagle carrier, and hurled His Sudarshana disc to cut off the head of the unrelenting crocodile. Gajendra was thus saved and awarded the highest position—service to God.

## Three Stages of Life

We can view this narration as an example of three phases of our existence in the material world. First, like the king of the elephants, we seek to enjoy pleasures. This stage is called SENSE GRATIFICATION. We discover that sense pleasures bring misery, but we hope to find relief with more pleasure pursuits. The result is an endless, complicated mesh of suffering. This next stage is called STRUGGLE or

SUFFERING. We pull and push our way through this world, paying a heavy price for all the sense gratification we engage in. We suffer as we struggle, and with no respite in sight, we delude ourselves into believing it's all part of the game called life. But our hearts hanker for unending happiness and relief from all suffering.

After many lifetimes of sense gratification and struggle, a battered and bruised living entity, if fortunate, finally surrenders to God. This is the SURRENDER stage, where, in a state of utter helplessness, the soul finds shelter in God's loving embrace.

Before taking to spiritual life, we live a material life centred on our own pleasures—sense gratification—where our mind drags us in different directions. Gajendra led a merry life of enjoyment; we too are oblivious to the harsh realities of this world. Somehow, a few of us come to a spiritual path and understand the seriousness of strict practices. Yet the mind, like the crocodile, drags us again into the lake of the material world. We want to get out of the grind of material life, but on our own, we are helpless. During this second stage—struggle—we try to control our minds. Previously, the mind hauled us around wherever it wanted to go, but now we seek to master it. As Gajendra struggled for centuries, we may endeavour for decades to gain mastery over our minds.

But it is obstinate and we suffer perpetually. Until, of course, we decide to enter the third stage—surrender—where we allow God to control our minds.

Stage 1: Sense gratification—the mind controls us.

Stage 2: Struggle—we try to control the mind.

Stage 3: Surrender—God takes charge of our mind.

When Gajendra realized he couldn't get out of suffering by his own methods, he gave up the struggle. This is also what Draupadi did. When she realized that cruel Duhsasana, goaded by his treacherous brother Duryodhana and their wily uncle Shakuni, was determined to disrobe her, when her own husbands were incapable of helping her, when she couldn't do anything on her own, she gave up the struggle and surrendered completely to Krishna.

## Spiritual Progress and the Need for Grace

An aspiring devotee on the path of Krishna consciousness (Bhakti Yoga) must reach the stage where the realization dawns that he or she can't achieve success on their own. To go back to God's kingdom, we need to access His grace, a power beyond our own. The advanced spiritual levels are not achieved by our endeavours; rather, they are awarded to us. And to receive grace, we need to surrender.

The main lesson from the story of Gajendra and the crocodile is that we have to move from sense gratification to struggle to finally surrender to God. It is this surrender that made Gajendra a hero in the pages of *Śrīmad-Bhāgavatam*.

One may wonder: If surrender is the final objective, why not surrender now? And what stops us from calling out to Krishna as Gajendra did?

## Why Can't We Surrender Now?

We lack the ability to helplessly call out to Krishna, like Gajendra did, for at least three reasons.

First, we are not aware that we are in the jaws of a crocodile called Maya—the material energy or our own wicked mind. A snake swallows a frog slowly, but surely. Even as the snake is gulping down the frog, the frog stretches out its tongue to catch a flying insect. Similarly, even as we are reduced to insignificance by all powerful time, we stay oblivious to our situation, busily catching insects daily in the form of our petty materialistic goals.

Second, even if we realize we are suffering in this world, we imagine that the crocodile of Maya will tire and eventually let us go. 'She can't keep biting me forever', we delude ourselves into thinking, 'she has to let go sometime.'

Sorry. She never lets go. She is never tired. The crocodile of Maya never sleeps.

We foolishly hope that things will get better in this world. A German saying, *Die Hoffnung stirbt zuletzt*, which translates as 'Hope dies last' has been around for a long time. Yet, despite our undying hope, in the material world, things never really improve. The crocodile of Maya will never relax. The only way to get relief is to surrender to Krishna completely.

A third reason why we don't surrender is that we falsely assure ourselves that we have in fact surrendered to God because we practice many rituals. But although we may learn scriptural verses or visit holy places, none of this can match the quality of the surrender of Gajendra, who cried out to Krishna for help. Until we take complete shelter in God, the crocodile will continue to bite us.

The only hope for the living entity suffering in the material world of repeated birth and death is to take complete shelter in God. Krishna, in the form of His holy names, can give us complete relief from suffering.

When God reciprocates with our sincere effort in chanting and prayers, and in our services to others, we'll see the crocodile of Maya as a blessing. Until then, we'll see and experience only suffering in this world.

And to reduce our suffering, we'll engage in sense gratification, and to afford the sense gratification, we'll endlessly struggle. It's thus a vicious downward cycle, which we can now end forever by just enjoying the sweetness of surrendering to God.

# Part II

# Chapter 2

# Why Should We Develop
Our Heart Space?

Is there a choice? Our lives would become a constant rollercoaster if we opted to reside in either of the other two houses: the House of Pleasure or the House of Struggle. It's essential to give ourselves a break!

Let's examine the three options available to us:

1. House of Pleasure: The allure and pitfalls of sensory gratification.
2. House of Problem Solving: The challenges and setbacks we encounter.
3. House of Peace/Home State: The benefits of dwelling in the Heart Space.

To clarify, it is only natural to seek the gratification of our senses. Additionally, it is reasonable to expect that we will face struggles throughout our lives; from our 'womb to the tomb', struggle is an inherent part of existence in this material world. However, in this section of the book, we propose dedicating daily time and energy to the surrender zone—the Heart Space. By spending some time each day in our Home State, we ensure our effectiveness as human beings and cultivate a sense of inner contentment.

Let's now dive into each of the three inner states of existence.

# Chapter 3

# Sense Gratification and the House of Pleasure

*Persons who are actually intelligent and philosophically inclined should endeavour only for that purposeful end which is not obtainable even by wandering from the topmost planet down to the lowest planet. As far as happiness derived from sense enjoyment is concerned, it can be obtained automatically in course of time, just as in course of time we obtain miseries even though we do not desire them.*

—*Śrīmad-Bhāgavatam* (1.5.18)

When we seek to satisfy our senses, our goal is to increase pleasure and reduce pain. However, life is not simply about experiencing constant pleasure. Pleasure and pain are two sides of the same coin in this material world. In fact, there is a pervasive law of pleasure in this world, similar to the law of gravitation. It states that everything we enjoy in this world will eventually bring equal or greater suffering.

Let's take a moment to consider our own bodies. Reflect on the different ways our bodies can bring us happiness. Write them down. Now, let's also acknowledge the various diseases and discomforts that our bodies can inflict upon us. Compare the two lists. Can you see the stark difference? The reality is that our bodies age, become vulnerable to diseases and eventually meet the inevitable fate of death, regardless of their initial beauty.

Now, let's address the question of when suffering begins. Some argue that discussions about spiritual life and death should be reserved for advanced age, while youth is a time for enjoyment and celebration. However, upon closer examination, we realize that suffering begins right from the moment of birth. Consider the number of paediatricians who have dedicated their lives to the care of infants and children. The existence of specialized medical care for children dates back to the fifth century BCE, as evident in ancient Ayurvedic texts and Greek writings from the first to the fourth century CE, which discuss specific childhood illnesses.[2] It is a sobering reality that people have suffered since time immemorial, and it begins right from birth. In fact, the third canto of *Śrīmad-Bhāgavatam* explores the plight of a child in the womb of its mother. It is rare to find a child emerging from the mother's womb with a smile or laughter; instead, every child enters this world crying out in pain.

As we progress through life, we encounter various challenges and responsibilities that require our attention and effort. From childhood onwards, we strive to address these issues, such as pursuing education, finding employment, managing loans and securing a place to live. Life is filled with numerous gaps that need to be filled, leading us to exist in what can be called the 'struggle zone.'

Constantly grappling with challenges can be exhausting, both mentally and physically. Therefore, amidst this ongoing struggle, we naturally seek moments of happiness and respite. This leads us to oscillate between what can be referred to as the 'pleasure house' and the 'problem-solving house'.

We often find ourselves in a perpetual cycle of moving between these two houses. We seek happiness and relief from the struggle by entering the pleasure house, but eventually, we must return to the problem-solving house to address the ongoing challenges and responsibilities that life presents.

The overall fallout of this lifestyle is insecurity and fear.

## The Fear Factor in Happiness

More than physical suffering, it is mental anxiety and insecurities that intensify as we grow older. The more we have, the more we need to ensure that we sustain our temporary possessions and fleeting position in this fragile world. A poor man worries about his next meal, while the powerful and wealthy are plagued by the fear of enemies. History is rife with infamous tales of individuals like Stalin, Mao and Mussolini who ruthlessly exterminated their closest aides out of fear that they would usurp their positions or gain popularity among the masses. In Vedic history, we find stories of Indra, the king of the higher planets, who was constantly anxious about losing his throne and would go to great lengths to eliminate any potential competitors. Consequently, true happiness remains elusive for both the impoverished and the affluent.

The reality of pleasure experiences in this world falls far short of what is depicted in the advertisements and disappointingly falls below our own expectations. Besides, the fleeting moments of pleasure often make us attached to our experience and fearful of losing it.

This fear impels us to struggle more, and when the struggle gets painful, we seek solace in sense gratification. Paradoxically, the more we indulge in such gratification, the stronger our attachments become, ultimately leading to even greater struggles. As a result, we find ourselves trapped in an unending cycle of suffering, constantly seeking temporary relief through sensory pleasures.

It is fear that fundamentally motivates human beings who are driven by a desire to enjoy.

## A Folktale from Bangladesh Emphatically Drives Home the Point:

Once upon a time, there lived a wealthy man who employed a poor maid servant. Her daily tasks included cleaning the house and washing her master's dishes. As she went about her duties, she couldn't help but gaze at the luxurious, cushioned bed in awe. Throughout her entire life, she had never experienced the comfort of sleeping on such a bed. Residing in the slums on the outskirts of town, she had grown accustomed to the hardness of the floor.

Every day, while tidying her master's bedroom, she would occasionally touch the bed and marvel at its softness. One fateful day, the master had to attend to urgent matters, leaving the maid alone at home to complete her chores. Seizing the opportunity, she couldn't resist the temptation and decided to lie down on the bed, longing to experience its comfort. Almost instantly, she drifted into a deep slumber.

An hour later, the master returned unexpectedly and was overcome with fury upon discovering his servant's audacity. 'How dare you sleep on my bed?' thundered the master. 'You uncouth woman! I shall teach you a lesson you'll never forget.'

The cruel master grabbed a whip and began mercilessly lashing the maid, causing her to scream out in pain. Believing that he was serving justice, the master continued to beat her relentlessly. Despite the agony she endured, an unexpected transformation occurred within the maid. Gradually, her screams turned into a smile and soon transformed into laughter. This only further infuriated the master, who couldn't comprehend how she could dare to laugh while being punished.

'What is the meaning of this laughter, you impudent woman?' roared the master, demanding an explanation.

With tears streaming down her face, the maid responded, 'Oh, master, I am filled with gratitude to God. I lay on your bed for just a few minutes, and I am now suffering so greatly. I can't help but wonder how much pain you must endure, as you have slept on this bed for years.'

The master's anger began to wane as her words struck a chord within him. In that moment, he realized the weight of his actions and the profound lesson the maid had unwittingly taught him. His heart softened, and he set aside the whip, realizing the depth of his own ignorance.

## Is Sense Gratification Harmful?

No! Sense gratification, in moderation, can add flavour to life, much like salt enhances the taste of food. However, excessive indulgence in sensory pleasures can lead to an unbalanced and unsatisfying existence.

Maintaining a healthy and balanced approach to gratification is crucial. In the Bhagavad Gita, Krishna declares, 'He who is regulated in his habits of eating, sleeping, recreation and work can mitigate all material pains by practising the yoga system' (6.17). This highlights the importance of moderation and self-regulation in our pursuit of pleasure.

However, when happiness becomes synonymous with the pursuit of sensory pleasures alone, it follows the law of diminishing returns. With each subsequent increase in indulgence, the pleasure derived from it diminishes, eventually leading to pain and dissatisfaction. For instance, if you are served a single gulab jamun (a syrupy Indian sweet), you may relish it. The second serving may bring additional pleasure, and perhaps after the fourth serving, you may declare that you've had enough. But if you were forced to consume more, each additional bite would become burdensome, and you would likely stop eating the sweet immediately.

However, a few days later, the craving may resurface with even greater intensity. Any pleasurable experience we enjoy tends to come back with stronger desires. Satisfying these cravings often requires struggling to obtain the necessary resources. As we indulge more, the eventual outcome is increased pain, as our bodies and senses have limited capacity to derive enjoyment from anything. Unfortunately, our desires do not diminish with age; instead, if we haven't learned to sublimate them, they tend to grow stronger as we get older. Consequently, our lives can become more miserable than those of animals.

## What Sets Us Apart from Animals?

While animals primarily operate based on their instinctual drives and survival instincts, humans have the capacity for higher understanding and spiritual realization. When we lack an understanding of our spiritual purpose and fail to aspire for a higher state of existence, we tend to oscillate between the pursuit of momentary pleasures and problem-solving, resulting in a tumultuous and unsettled life.

One significant distinction is our ability to transcend mere material desires and seek a deeper meaning for our existence. Animals are driven by basic instincts such as eating, sleeping, sex and self-preservation (defence). However, humans, if properly guided, can rise above these primal instincts and explore higher dimensions of life.

If we closely observe animals, we can see that they live in a constant state of fear and struggle. For instance, consider a hen pecking at her food. She remains vigilant, constantly scanning her surroundings, wary of a potential threat from a lurking cat. Similarly, in the streets, we may witness dogs engaging in fights and pursuits to mate with a female. Humans, on the other hand, exhibit different behaviour in these areas. When we eat, we don't experience fear of being attacked, and in a civilized society, we don't have other individuals fighting or lusting after our partners. Animals fulfil their basic needs in 'nasty and unpleasant conditions', as described by Srila Prabhupada in his book, *Sri Ishopanishad*.

> There are swine, dogs, camels, asses, etc., whose economic necessities are just as important to them as ours are to us, but the economic problems of these animals are solved only under nasty and unpleasant conditions. The human being is given all facilities for a comfortable life by the laws of nature because the human form of life is more important and valuable than animal life. Why is man given a better life than that of the swine and other animals? Why is a highly placed government servant given better facilities than those of an ordinary clerk? The answer is that a highly placed officer has to discharge duties of a higher nature. Similarly, the duties human beings have

*to perform are higher than those of animals, who are always*
*engaged in simply feeding their hungry stomachs.*[3]

However, if humans refuse to seek a life beyond mere sense gratification and struggle, we risk devolving into nothing more than well-dressed, polished and sophisticated two-legged animals. We regress to lower stages of consciousness, neglecting our unique capacity to explore and realize our spiritual potential.

## The Different Levels of Consciousness

According to the Vedic literature, there are five stages of consciousness:

### 1. *Avrata*—Covered Consciousness

The Vedic books of wisdom proclaimed thousands of years ago that even plants and trees possess life. However, their consciousness is veiled, and their perception of pleasure and pain is highly limited. This is why we observe trees enduring hours of rain and extreme weather conditions without complaint.

### 2. *Sankuchita*—Constricted Consciousness

Animals and birds possess a higher level of consciousness compared to plants. They can perceive pleasure and pain to a greater extent and exhibit intelligence similar to humans. For instance, a sneaky cat might venture into the kitchen to drink milk when no one is around. However, their thoughts are primarily centred on basic instincts such as eating, sleeping, mating and defending.

Once, in our ashram, the monastery of monks, each of us was given a couple of hangers to hang our shirts for drying on the open terrace. However, over time, all fifty residents lost their hangers. We wondered who could have stolen them, and as weeks passed, we forgot about the incident.

One day, while on the terrace, I noticed a beautiful nest perched on the top branch of a tree facing the ashram. To my astonishment, the nest was entirely constructed from our cloth hangers. I called the other residents, and together, we marvelled at the ingenuity of these simple birds.

Where did these birds learn to build a nest, let alone one made of hangers? We have never heard of any bird studying civil engineering at the prestigious Indian Institute of Technology. This incident highlights the intelligence present in animals and birds. However, the key distinction is that they are unable to expand their thinking or employ their intelligence beyond the four basic instincts of eating, sleeping, sex life and self-defence.

It becomes evident that humans, too, utilize their intelligence to engage in these activities, albeit in a more complex manner. However, we have the potential to transcend these basic propensities and pursue higher endeavours.

## 3. *Mukulita*—Blossoming Consciousness

Human beings are in this category, as we possess a consciousness that can be likened to a bud, holding the potential to blossom into a beautiful flower. Unlike animals, humans possess the capacity to inquire about birth and death, as well as explore the purpose of life.

Through sincere inquiry and introspection, we can discover answers to the most perplexing questions that arise in our lives. We have the ability to transcend the pursuit of mere bodily pleasures and the daily struggle to fulfil our desires. Our existence encompasses more than the basic instincts of eating, sleeping, sex and defending. As humans, we possess an innate ability to tap into this higher potential.

### 4. *Vikasita*—Developed consciousness and 5. *Purna Vikasita*—Fully evolved consciousness

These two states represent the pinnacle of advanced consciousness, where an individual's sense of identity merges with the universe and they recognize themselves as servants of God. In this state, they perceive their oneness with divinity and find deep contentment in being instruments of God, spreading joy and hope in the lives of others. They perceive the presence of God everywhere and in everything.

An incident involving Srila Prabhupada beautifully exemplifies this perspective. Once, while strolling in a garden with a few disciples, a pleasant yet cold wind blew. One of the students offered a shawl for Srila Prabhupada to keep warm. However, he graciously declined it and spontaneously expressed that the gentle breeze was Krishna's embrace. As he sat on the soft grass, another devotee quickly arranged a cushioned seat for his spiritual master. Again, Srila Prabhupada dismissed it, remarking that he was already seated on God's lap. This incident illustrates Srila Prabhupada's ability to perceive God both as a person and as the essence permeating all of creation.

## Ascending the Levels of Consciousness

As we ascend the ladder of consciousness, we gradually enter the realm of the Heart Space, where we begin to perceive the presence of God in our daily lives. By nurturing qualities like appreciation and gratitude, we shift our mindset from scarcity and fear to one of abundance.

Among the four fundamental propensities shared with animals, fear stands out prominently. While we can only eat until our stomachs are full, sleep for a limited number of hours and have sex a few times until the desire invades again at another time, fear and the instinct to defend persist constantly. It's ubiquitous—fear drives us to work, travel, earn, save and even engage in conflicts. Even when we are not experiencing overt fear from external sources, our subconscious minds harbour insecurities and anxieties that can compromise our well-being by weakening our immune systems.

Hence, *Śrīmad-Bhāgavatam* and other Vedic scriptures implore humans to seek a life that transcends struggle and sense gratification, which are basically driven by fear. It behoves us to tap into this human endowment and perfect our lives. We have superior intelligence as compared to the animals, which is evident when a man of modest stature and meagre physical strength is able to encage ferocious lions and tame wild elephants. Yet, when our intelligence is used for fulfilling only our primal needs, we are no different from animals.

## Pleasure Seeking Is Eventually Pain-Giving

To seek pleasure for the body is natural for human beings. However, it is important to recognize that seeking pleasure alone is a poor substitute for true happiness, which encompasses a much richer experience beyond the limitations of our senses.

Recently, during my morning walk, a lady wearing a strong perfume passed by me from the opposite direction. For a brief moment, the fragrance assaulted my senses, but it was quickly overshadowed by the foul smell emanating from unattended garbage on the streets. A few minutes later, I arrived at a garden where the staff was watering the rose plants. The fragrance of the damp earth combined with the sight of beautiful fruit-bearing trees touched me on a deeper level, providing a more meaningful experience.

It is true that a captivating dance number on a mobile screen can temporarily elevate our dopamine levels, but engaging in the chanting and dancing of the Holy Names of Krishna during kirtans can offer us a more fulfilling experience. While our taste buds may be aroused by the sight or smell of crunchy, spicy Indian snacks topped with tamarind chutney, true satisfaction of the palate is discovered when we mindfully savour our daily meals consisting of chapatis, vegetables, rice and dal. Nature offers experiences that surpass the fleeting relief of our pleasure pursuits, but to access them, we must make healthy choices in our diet, associations and lifestyle.

Our pursuit of pleasure often acts as a painkiller, providing temporary relief from the struggles of our daily lives. It is natural to seek such respite, but the problem arises when we substitute the painkiller for genuine healing. Let's imagine a scenario where a friend develops chest pain and consults a doctor. The doctor prescribes a healthy regimen of exercise and a balanced diet. However, instead of following the prescribed lifestyle, our friend discovers a cheap painkiller that instantly relieves the chest pain. It becomes convenient for him to simply pop a painkiller whenever the pain arises, avoiding the disciplined lifestyle recommended by the doctor.

What do you think would be his fate? After some time, the painkiller will no longer provide relief and he may need to take two pills. Eventually, even half a dozen painkillers will fail to alleviate the pain. Similarly, seeking sensory gratification may initially offer some respite from our suffering, but if we neglect the nourishment of our Heart Space, these temporary pleasures will prove ineffective. Despite indulging in a multitude of sensory pursuits, we will continue to feel an inner hollowness.

## Modern Painkillers: Smartphones and Social Media

My friend used to proudly claim that he wasn't addicted to his smartphone and knew how to use his gadgets wisely. However, he recently came to the realization that whenever he faced challenges at work or experienced failed relationships, he would spend an excessive amount of time on social media. It dawned on him that apps like WhatsApp, Instagram and Facebook served as his personal 'painkiller'. The act of endlessly scrolling through these apps and getting lost in videos provided him with temporary relief. It became a means for him to escape from his miserable reality. Engaging in mindless chats and watching meaningless videos on his phone seemed to be the modern equivalent of drowning one's sorrows with alcohol. Instead of going to a bar, people now had the option to grab their tablets and further indulge in a life of denial.

In today's age, the internet is filled with literature and research studies that expose how social media apps employ algorithms specifically designed to keep users glued to their smartphone screens. It delivers a similar rush to that of a slot machine, as users eagerly anticipate a virtual 'jackpot'. Thus, we now find both gambling and alcohol-like effects bundled together in one place. However, the instant surge of dopamine and pleasure derived from our phones isn't as harmless as it appears. It rewires our brains and robs us of the genuine happiness that can be found in simple, real-world experiences. For example, watching a beautiful rain shower on an electronic screen may evoke some excitement, but it pales in comparison to the fulfilment one could derive from witnessing the actual rain outside their window. Similarly, steamy sex scenes in a web series are designed to titillate our senses, but can they ever replace the depth and intimacy of a meaningful relationship with a loved one? As we grapple with challenges in the real world and seek gratification in the virtual realm, we gradually transform into zombies. Slowly but surely, we disconnect from genuine real-life experiences and get hooked on the illusory world of flashing images.

## Overcoming the Challenges of the Ever Dissatisfied Mind

The mind constantly seeks relief from suffering. For example, imagine the overcrowded local trains in Mumbai, where hundreds of people squeeze into a space meant for a fraction of that number. In such situations, finding a seat, even if it's a rare occurrence, brings immense relief. Similarly, a boxer who gets a break between rounds feels relief because he is no longer being hit. These instances represent a shift from a state of constant suffering to a momentary respite.

However, living solely for sensory gratification or relief can lead to disappointment. Sensory pleasures are often less fulfilling than anticipated or promised, and they are transient. Even if we attain something we desire, the enjoyment it brings doesn't last long and it is often accompanied by pain. Additionally, most worldly happiness is relative and changes according to our circumstances. For example, entering an air-conditioned room after being stuck in a noisy and hot traffic jam can offer great relief. However, after some time, the effect wears off and the mind continues to find reasons to complain and seek further relief through sense gratification. This continuous struggle for enjoyment is an inherent part of the material realm.

One hundred twenty years ago, the Taj Mahal hotel in Mumbai advertised in newspapers that its special rooms were equipped with a fan to provide cooling comfort. The advertisement featured an image of a three-blade fan, with a joyful woman smiling below. What was once considered a luxury has now become a necessity. Still, despite the abundance of conveniences and comforts available today, the mind's incessant chatter continues unabated. It expertly highlights what is lacking in our lives or how the world seems to be spiralling into chaos. Paradoxically, the same mind seeks solace from this constant grumbling through acts of sensory indulgence. As a result, we find ourselves trapped in an unending cycle of struggle and fleeting enjoyment.

In modern times, a new phenomenon has emerged—the pursuit of happiness in the unreal or virtual world. Unlike sightseeing at landmarks, which is a real experience, modern forms of entertainment, such as complex storylines, music videos or movies viewed on electronic screens, transport us to non-existent landscapes filled with gory murders and explicit scenes. Although these experiences are unreal, their impact on our consciousness is real and long-lasting.

Thus, in the twenty-first century, there are three realms where people seek happiness: the unreal or virtual world, the real but temporary world and the spiritual realm. While spiritual teachers of the past helped individuals transition from the temporary to the eternal, the present challenge lies in guiding people to move from the illusory world of smartphones and virtual experiences to at least engaging with the temporary world. Only then can they gradually rise to the spiritual dimension of happiness.

Living in the real world and cherishing genuine interactions with others is a significant achievement in itself. Amidst the struggles and joys of this tangible reality, one may develop a desire to transcend the dualities of pain and pleasure, leading to the initiation of a spiritual quest. However, breaking free from the clutches of the virtual world, which numbs our authentic emotions, is a necessary first step for all these transformative experiences to manifest.

# Chapter 4

## Struggles in the House of Problem-Solving

The mind, not content with seeking pleasure alone, also gravitates towards suffering. It thrives on ranting, moaning and indulging in a multitude of undesirable emotions such as hurt, pain, melancholy, judgements, prejudices, fear and anger, among others.

An illustrative incident sheds light on this phenomenon. Years ago, a wealthy man from Mumbai expressed his desire to forsake his riches and embrace a peaceful life in Khirsu, a lesser-known village in Uttarakhand, northern India. Intrigued, a reporter ventured to the village and encountered a humble villager in this rustic and charming vacation spot. Curious, the reporter inquired about the man's aspirations. To the reporter's surprise, the villager confessed, 'I dream of someday going to Mumbai and amassing wealth in that glamorous city.'

## The Choice of Dissatisfaction

When life in the realm of struggle becomes our default setting, we consciously choose to remain dissatisfied. We perpetually seek to fill perceived voids in our lives and, consequently, fail to acknowledge and appreciate our blessings. Our focus remains fixated on comparisons with others and longing for what they possess.

I once heard a story in our monastery that beautifully illustrates this wisdom.

*A crow, plagued by despondency, lamented, 'I am neither beautiful nor capable of singing melodiously. I am merely a dirty scavenger, perpetually shunned by people.' At that moment, the crow caught sight of a magnificent swan and exclaimed, 'Oh, how captivating you are! With your sparkling white feathers and graceful stride, you reside in stunning lakes adorned with blooming lotuses, admired by all.' Humbly, the swan lowered its head and expressed regret, saying, 'Dear friend, I am but a plain, unremarkable white bird. However, consider the parrot! He is resplendently green, with a reddish beak and a melodious voice, making him the preferred choice. Humans adore keeping parrots as pets, pampering them excessively.' The crow subsequently encountered a parrot and showered praise upon him, claiming he was the most fortunate bird of all. 'I feel incomplete,' confessed the parrot, 'I envy the multi-coloured feathers of a peacock. Undoubtedly, it is the epitome of beauty. When it spreads its feathers and dances in the rain, it creates the most mesmerizing spectacle.' Intrigued, the crow sought out the seemingly blessed peacock and was astonished to find that it, too, felt hopeless in its existence. 'I have no privacy; people relentlessly pursue me, hunters poach my feathers and I am sold in zoos,' lamented the peacock. 'You are the luckiest; nobody disturbs you. How I wish I were a carefree, contented crow, soaring freely like you!'*

In Mumbai, numerous families reside in simple tenement-style buildings known as 'chawls'. While the affluent occupy apartments or their own bungalows, they often lead lives marked by solitude and loneliness. In contrast, chawl residents experience greater social interactions and partake in community festivals. However, influenced by depictions in movies where the wealthy drive flashy cars and have beautiful partners, a contented chawl resident may still feel inadequate and yearn to attain the status of the on-screen heroes he idolizes. Thus, the simple and poor 'fans' remain ever dissatisfied, forever chasing the proverbial carrot that remains just out of reach, like a desperate donkey. Meanwhile, the very heroes they worship harbour their own insecurities and fears. Both the hero and the fan struggle in this world. And amidst it all, we ponder, 'Why am I not happy?'

## The 'Gain' vs 'Gaps' Consciousness

Living solely in the realm of struggle and seeking immediate gratification denies us true peace. While there may be fleeting satisfaction in fulfilling our senses, the underlying inadequacies and gaps persistently haunt us. But when we enter the peaceful shelter zone, we also tap into the realm of gain. The difference between the consciousness of 'gaps' and 'gains' is profound.

An individual immersed in constant struggle primarily focuses on the gaps in their life—what they have yet to achieve or acquire. This mindset prevents them from finding peace and embracing a grateful celebration of life. On the other hand, someone residing in the shelter zone begins to perceive the gains—the blessings they have received. This shift in consciousness brings contentment.

An anecdote better illustrates this concept. Once, a friend decided to surprise his family by bringing home some special pizzas from our Govinda's restaurant. When he revealed his gifts, his younger daughter was overjoyed, but the older one exclaimed, 'Dad, this isn't my favourite pizza. You know I love the ones with jalapeños.' The younger child naturally embraced the 'gain' space, while the older child dwelled in the 'gap'. She failed to recognize that it was a delightful surprise and a gain. Her scarcity mindset prevented her from appreciating the beauty of life.

## Are You a Struggle Addict?

When we constantly reside in the struggle zone, we yearn to reach a place or situation we believe will bring us happiness. Ironically, even if we were to reach such a state, we would continue to struggle because we lack the ability to recognize happiness. Struggling is all we know. In fact, when we do experience moments of peace, we question ourselves, 'Why do I feel so peaceful? What is wrong? I must do something.' Peace discomforts a struggle addict.

During my early days as a monk apprentice, I would chant my Japa meditation with the fervour and enthusiasm of a monk seeking to conquer the spiritual realm. I engaged in distracted sessions, vigorously shaking my head while fingering my chanting beads, hoping that with greater concentration, I would soon find God. I thought, 'Krishna is here somewhere and I will soon attain Him.' One day, during yet another intense meditation session, I noticed a senior congregation leader quietly chanting at a distance, observing me curiously. After the session ended and the bells rang, he humbly approached me and inquired about my activities during the two-hour session. I matter-of-factly replied that I was attempting to control my mind. Probing further, he asked, 'Is it such a great struggle?' I answered, 'Yes, I struggle to attain Krishna and these battles with my mind will purify me and bring me closer to God.' He sighed and looked away, disappointed. Perplexed, I asked if I had said something wrong.

He responded, 'Well, no, not really', with a wry smile. 'I spend the entire week struggling at work, at home and in my relationships. I look forward to coming to the temple on Sundays, seeking shelter. But when I arrive here, I see monks like you, who reside here, also struggling. It saddens me to realize that you are just as miserable as I am.'

That moment was an epiphany for me. I instantly recognized that my practice was fundamentally flawed. I needed to embrace peace and dwell in the shelter zone, avoiding unnecessary struggles. What the outside world yearned to achieve by coming to the temple, I already possessed as a gift. My journey had reached its destination, yet due to my habit of residing in the struggle zone, I failed to recognize my happiness and the need to gratefully connect with God.

Another friend confided in me that whenever he felt low and sad, he eagerly anticipated his Sunday visits to the temple. He imagined himself entering the peaceful ambiance of the temple, associating with other monks and congregation members, and finding shelter. This thought provided him the strength to immerse himself in his struggle-filled life. However, he admitted that when he actually visited the temple, he felt restless. I suggested that perhaps he was addicted to living in the 'gap'—constantly planning for the following week and unable to be happy in the present moment. He needed to discover 'peace' in his workplace and at home as well. Only then would he fully appreciate the spiritual energy present in the temple atmosphere. Otherwise, he would persistently struggle, remain agitated and pursue an imaginary state of happiness. He needed to release the struggle and accept the present.

Our inability to accept our current circumstances and view them as complete constantly agitates us. We mistakenly equate happiness with sensory stimulation. Therefore, when we are not excited, we assume we are unhappy and conclude that something is wrong with our lives. And so, to rectify the perceived wrong, we continue to struggle.

## The Happiness-Obsessed Generation

Russ Harris, the author of *The Happiness Trap*, argues that we are a generation obsessed with happiness, believing that it is our inherent right to be happy at all times.[4] However, the reality of the human psyche paints a different picture. Happiness is not something we can always control; it is a gift we receive. Until about a century ago, various cultures viewed happiness as divinely ordained, with our responsibility being to fulfil our duties well. Life was centred on purpose and whether happiness accompanied it or not was uncertain.

In contrast to the past, today's mindset is centred around an insistent pursuit of happiness. We are willing to go to great lengths to achieve this elusive state of mind, even resorting to creating purpose statements. Interestingly, our grandparents never had such formal declarations, yet their lives seamlessly aligned with the universal principles of 'be good' and 'do well to others.' They found contentment and possessed the ability to gracefully and gratefully endure life's extremes, such as adverse weather, deaths, losses and more. However, our generation, despite having numerous conveniences, lacks the same level of tolerance. When we find ourselves unhappy, we often jump to the conclusion that something must be wrong with us.

A recent incident made me reflect on this issue. I was sitting on a bench in a garden when a friend approached me, asking if I could attend a meeting later that evening. I honestly replied that I couldn't because I was feeling a little sad about certain developments in my personal life and preferred to be alone for a few hours. He wanted to offer empathy, but I assured him that I was fine and that it wasn't a severe situation. Perplexed, he asked how someone like me, a senior spiritual practitioner, couldn't be happy all the time. I responded by saying, 'Well, I am a human being first and it's okay to feel sad. I will be alright tomorrow morning.'

Just as seasons transition from summer to monsoon and winter arrives unasked, our emotions also undergo constant change. In fact, our feelings fluctuate daily, often shifting multiple times within a single day. Consider asking any mother if she loves her child and she will likely affirm this without hesitation. However, if you inquire whether she is always 'happy' with her child, you will discover a range of different emotions that she experiences in relation to her offspring. These emotions may include frustration, anger and restlessness, as well as moments of happiness. Life is a tapestry woven with diverse emotions and to lead fulfilling lives, we must find peace within ourselves and embrace the many waves of emotional states that rise and fall within our inner world.

It is essential to cultivate a healthy Heart Space where we can find inner anchorage. This state of shelter allows us to navigate through life's vicissitudes with greater depth. In a world that promises instant gratification, accepting setbacks is often unpopular. Rather than tolerating the inevitable ups and downs of life, many of us prefer to quickly change external circumstances and relationships.

Nonetheless, does this constant pursuit of new situations guarantee happiness? We convince ourselves that happiness is just around the corner or persuade ourselves that life is inherently unpredictable. This is not necessarily tolerance or wisdom; it may merely reflect frustrated resignation or a denial of suffering. It's our actions that speak volumes—many seek temporary relief to soothe their bruised egos and minds, with more instant gratification. So, they continue an endless struggle—a game they can never win.

It's akin to being forced into a boxing ring and repeatedly beaten by a stronger opponent. You may desire to quit the game, but leaving the ring is not an option and winning seems unattainable. For eternal strugglers, life becomes a game they can't win and can't quit playing!

## Case Study from History: Living in the Sense Gratification and Struggle House

At the tender age of eleven, Babur ascended to the throne of Fergana Valley, located in present-day Uzbekistan. However, his true passions resided in the realms of poetry, art, music and gardening. Despite his inclination towards these peaceful pursuits that were his Shelter House (his Home State), Babur found himself drawn to the notorious legacies of his ancestors. His father's lineage traced back to the fearsome Timur, while his mother's ancestry linked him to the dreaded Genghis Khan. Though it was not his natural calling, Babur decided to follow in their footsteps, influenced by the reputation these conquerors had garnered for their brutalities and merciless massacres of innocent civilians. Consequently, as young and impressionable as he was, Babur nurtured similar ambitions.

Filled with desires, Babur's heart yearned to conquer Samarkand, the birthplace of Timur, and thus he embarked on his journey to seek power. After a tremendous struggle, at the age of fifteen, Babur managed to seize control of Samarkand, but his triumph was short-lived, as he lost it within a few months. Meanwhile, in his absence, his brother seized power in their native Fergana Valley, leaving Babur without a kingdom. Despite numerous attempts to reclaim Samarkand, Babur faced constant failures and his obsession with regaining the city grew.

Eventually, frustrated and disheartened, Babur returned to Fergana, hoping to reclaim his lost kingdom. Unfortunately, fate dealt him another harsh blow and he suffered a resounding defeat. Left with no other choice, Babur escaped with a small group of loyal followers and sought refuge in the rugged mountains of Central Asia, relying on the hospitality of local tribes. Enduring poverty and humiliation, Babur gradually lost hope of ever reclaiming his beloved homeland. And this meant he was going further away from his Heart Space.

## Rejecting the Inner Calling: Babur's Struggles and Pursuit of Power

Babur writes in his memoirs that he had an ascetic spiritual tendency that was unnatural amongst his war mongering clan. One would then imagine that this failure as a warrior was a good time for him to reflect and pursue his inner calling.

Yet, instead of embracing his spiritual side, he succumbed to the prevailing trend of pederasty, a practice favoured by the Central Asian aristocracy of that time. He developed a strong infatuation for a young sixteen-year-old boy and also entered into several marriages. In a life dominated by bisexual relationships and a relentless pursuit of power, Babur buried his asceticism and humanity.

Gradually, Babur shifted his focus towards building a formidable army and seeking his fortune elsewhere. He successfully captured Afghanistan, but remained disdainful of the vices and luxuries prevalent in Herat and Kabul. He found liquor and intoxicants repulsive, distancing himself from such indulgences.

Babur's gaze then turned towards India, where the northern regions were under the rule of Ibrahim Lodi. Invited by those who opposed Lodi, Babur attempted to conquer Delhi. However, he faced initial failures. In 1524, when his army was defeated by Lodi, Babur responded by inflicting devastating damage upon the city of Lahore, resulting in the loss of countless innocent lives. Two years later, equipped with artillery and cannons that were unknown to the Indian Army at the time, Babur emerged victorious in the first Battle of Panipat, defeating Lodi. He further defeated Rana Sangha of Mewar, once again leveraging his superior artillery. With these victories, Babur became the undisputed ruler of northern India.

## Heart Space Living Is the Right Thing to Do

One might assume that Babur now had ample reasons to be content. But, ironically, he now began to drink, host wine parties and take opium and other narcotics. And still, this newfound lifestyle—of sense gratification and constant struggle—did not bring him happiness. Historian Abraham Eraly reveals that even amidst his success in India, Babur lamented his failure to reclaim Samarkand. His heart longed for what he could not attain elsewhere. Babur's life and exploits resonate with a verse from the Bhagavad Gita (18.34): 'But that determination by which one clings to selfish results in religion, economic development and egoistic gratification is of the nature of passion.'

Understanding why Babur wasn't content isn't a challenging task. The Greek philosopher Epictetus provides the answer: 'Happiness and personal fulfilment are the natural consequences of doing the right thing.'

## The Divergent Paths: Babur's Missed Opportunity for Heart Space Living

Amidst Babur's self-perception as a holy warrior of Islam, an era of religious harmony was unfolding in India with the emergence of Guru Nanak, the founder of Sikhism. In contrast to Babur's concept of jihad, India witnessed the growth of Vaishnavism, a branch of Hinduism that emphasized peace and the love of God. The humble Vaishnava saints became messengers of peace, offering a message of harmony. While Babur excelled in devising military strategies, his victories did not bring him true happiness. He was at last doing things right and that gave him victories, but was he doing the right things?

Babur had his chance to be a saint; he simply had to follow his inner calling. He could have been a messenger of peace and love, but he lost it. Ironically, while he conquered India, he missed the essence of Indian spirituality and suffered a profound internal defeat. His ambition and determination led to great external triumphs, but at what cost? Frederick Douglass, the influential African–American social reformer of the eighteenth century, eloquently appealed to our conscience when he said, 'I prefer to be true to myself, even at the hazard of incurring the ridicule of others, rather than to be false and incur my own abhorrence.'

We are constantly faced with distractions and temptations, and it's not easy to follow our inner calling. Especially when the soft inner voice implores us to be an agent of positivity but our raging mind and senses, impelled by the ego, direct us to do the wrong things. Conscience is that still, small voice that is sometimes too loud for our comfort. Yet, if we show courage and determination to follow the right but difficult path, we may be pleasantly surprised to see that we reach a beautiful destination. The correct choices always yield the right results. And the strength to make the correct choices comes when we live in the Heart Space.

The truth is that, deep down, we always know the right thing to do. The toughest part is actually doing it. While Babur died long before he was buried, we can choose to live and love.

# Chapter 5

## Shelter in the Heart Space

### Finding Peace in Chaos: A Journey of Surrender and Resilience

Amidst the outbreak of the Covid-19 pandemic in 2020, I found myself stranded in my mother's house, nestled in a small coastal town in southern India. The government had imposed a strict lockdown, confining us within the walls of our home. During those days, my mother and I would devote a few hours each day to chanting, reading scriptures and praying together. Within the confines of our house, we created our own sanctuary, our Home State.

One fateful night, a cyclone struck, unleashing heavy rains and plunging us into darkness as the power went out. The fierce winds whipped the coconut trees into a wild dance, and I witnessed a long snake fall from the roof, writhing in pain as it slithered away. My mosquito net was torn away and the clothes I had hung out to dry vanished with the gusts. The thunderous thuds of falling trees and the violent shaking of our house threatened to alter the landscape, as if the winds desired to uproot our dwelling completely. Fear and chaos enveloped the atmosphere, but I held tightly onto my mother's hand, who was bedridden and unable to leave the house. Helplessness loomed over us like the sword of Damocles.

In that moment, a wave of peace washed over my consciousness. I looked at my mother and she smiled back at me, uttering the words, 'Son, if this is it, let it be so.' Quietly, she offered her prayers and I felt a strange calmness and reassurance. I realized that I was not merely this physical body and that my life extended beyond the pandemonium surrounding me. I seamlessly let go of control, placing my trust in the universe to guide us. It was an act of surrender and a tangible peace pervaded the atmosphere.

Eventually, the storm subsided and we quietly set about restoring order within our home. It was in that moment of reorganization that I discovered an inner reservoir of fortitude and patience I hadn't known existed within me. Reflecting upon the experience in my journal, I came to understand the profound impact of cultivating a daily practice of connecting with our Heart Space. This practice had helped us avoid impulsive reactions, enabling us to maintain sobriety and inner peace. Furthermore, I realized that our ability to bounce back from life's unexpected challenges is deeply influenced by the development of our Home State and the amount of time we invest in nurturing it.

In the face of chaos, I found solace and resilience through surrender and the cultivation of inner strength. The storm had tested us, but it had also revealed the power of a peaceful heart.

## The Inner Cushion: Nurturing Our Home State

You are leading a normal life with daily routines and monotonous tasks to do. Your emotional stability, if it could be quantified on a scale of one to ten, is at level five. Your problems and worries are at level two. You seem to be coasting along your regular life and you seem to be effective because you are situated above your worries. Suddenly, a phone call from a loved one disturbs you or your child has met with a serious accident (God forbid!) or you lost your savings in a bad investment. The worry graph suddenly jumps to level seven—two levels higher than your level of sanity. You lack the wherewithal to navigate the crisis; you breakdown, overwhelmed by the emotional tsunami.

On the other hand, if you have cultivated a daily practice of living in the Heart Space for a dedicated period of time, your emotional baseline elevates to level nine—a significant seven levels above your daily worries. When faced with sudden bad news, you discover a protective cushion within, shielding your emotional state. The deposits in your mental account remain abundant compared to the withdrawals caused by the tragedy.

Home State living creates this buffer in your inner world. It strengthens your capacity to cope with the fluctuations of fortune, shielding you from the extreme mood swings that often accompany an emotional roller coaster.

## We Don't Die

We are not bound by death. The true essence of ourselves, beyond the limitations of this physical body and mind, is described in the ancient Indian Vedas as Brahman—the eternal, undying reality. The Vedas also refer to this state as the essence of everything, or the Brahman. It is the singular, eternal truth amidst a world of illusions and transience.

Intuitively, we recognize the impermanence of everything around us, which is why we often feel dissatisfied and incomplete, despite the abundance of objects to enjoy or the multitude of activities to keep us occupied. Nothing in this world can bring us lasting happiness because everything is subject to destruction, while our true selves, the 'I', never age or deteriorate. We may not always be able to articulate this longing, but the yearning for something unending and eternal remains within us. This is why we are naturally drawn to mountains, oceans and forests—things that appear to our senses as enduring. Poets find inspiration in the moon, philosophers lose themselves in contemplation of the stars and even those caught up in the daily struggles of material life find solace in witnessing the rising and setting sun. These experiences are a result of our inner selves, which never truly die, finding a connection with another immortal reality in nature. The sun, moon and stars have witnessed the passing of generations, including our great-grandfathers. They observed the Mahabharata war and the arrival of Shankaracharya. They have witnessed remarkable individuals and catastrophic events throughout the millennia. Similarly, we, trapped within these mortal bodies, are eternal, fully conscious and blissful. Unbeknownst to us, it is the eternity of Brahman that we seek during our journey in this world. The tranquillity we experience in nature merely beckons our souls to enter the realm of eternity.

If you are tormented by questions such as who you are or the meaning of it all or if you contemplate what is truly real in this world and your place within the vast cosmos, you are on a spiritual quest. Have you ever pondered the nature of your thoughts? Where does intelligence originate from? Is there something beyond form and labels?

The answer that encompasses all these questions is Brahman—the eternal reality transcending all material existence and limitations. Whether in the grand scope of the universe or within our own microcosmic realm, Brahman shapes our resilience and happiness. As we face storms of suffering from both internal and external sources, it is our state of Brahman—the authentic 'I', the unchanging and observing self—that guarantees profound fulfilment and joy.

## Stability–Clarity–Love: The Three Principles that Catapults Us to the Eternal Space

Let's now translate this abstract phenomenon called Brahman to our daily lives.

Brahman is a state characterized by 'stability–clarity–love'. In Vedic terminology, they are referred to as 'satcitananda', where the word Sat represents eternity, a state of balance and equilibrium. Cit signifies consciousness or awareness, while Ananda represents pure bliss experienced when one feels deeply loved. Thus, the soul is also described in Vedic scriptures as satcitananda—eternal (or stability), fully aware (clarity) and blissful (love).

To experience lasting happiness, we simply need to nurture three essential aspects—the triangle of stability, clarity and love. The more time we spend in our Heart Space, the greater our chances of anchoring ourselves in stability, clarity and love.

I once knew a corporate professional with a lucrative salary who confessed to drinking and partying while feeling an ever-growing emptiness with age. Despite owning a grand house and having substantial savings, he felt a sense of instability in life because his wife had chosen another man. He described himself as a ship without a rudder, confused about his goals and unsure about what would truly make him happy.

Gradually, with spiritual association and meditation practices, he discovered his Home State, which was offering kindness and empathy to others, reading life-enhancing literature and practising daily yoga. When he genuinely served or expanded his mind through the study of good books and leading a sattvic lifestyle of yoga and morning walks, he felt once again connected to himself. He had chosen to simplify his life. There was more awareness in his life now and that, in turn, led to more stability and self-love.

Initially, he denied his suffering and used spiritual practices as a means to escape his pain and evade responsibility for his life. Yet, with consistent dedication, he learned to accept his broken heart and mended it through practices that guaranteed stability, clarity and love, regardless of external circumstances. These three principles are not dependent on the external world; a decaying body and mortal relationships cannot provide us with stability. Clarity and love transcend the pursuit of mere mental pleasure.

Only a person who has satisfied his hunger can serve food to others. Similarly, the more we spend time in meditation and feel loved by God, the more we can give love to this world. This creates a cyclical effect—we receive more love when we give without expectations and we transcend our reliance on this ephemeral world when our source of shelter is beyond temporary relationships.

In our spiritual community, known as ISKCON, members begin to experience love beyond the confines of the body and mind by connecting with Krishna—the Supreme Personality of Godhead, as described in Vedic scriptures. Chanting the Hare Krishna mantra helps spiritual practitioners feel loved, and dwelling in this space cultivates awareness or clarity. Through awareness of our separate existence from the transient world, we reside in a state of stability.

This is the embodiment of satcitananda—stability, clarity and love in action. It represents the realization of the Home State or Brahman in the twenty-first century, reminiscent of the pursuit that inspired great sages of the past to renounce worldly attachments and seek self-realization.

## Does the Heart Space Guarantee Immunity from Suffering?

No! But it offers a sanctuary.

Lovers of God also suffer. No one is spared! Yet there is a distinct difference. Krishna, the Super Soul residing in our hearts, guides and nourishes us, providing a deeply fulfilling Home State experience. As we endure external suffering, just like anyone else in the world, we undergo a spiritual transformation. The difference lies in being loved by a caring parent, even when the world throws terrible surprises at us.

Imagine a child playing a ball game outside his house and accidentally breaking a neighbour's window. The neighbour, a stern lady, steps out to punish the child. In that very moment, the boy's mother rushes out and grabs hold of her son, delivering a hard slap. The child cries at his mother's harsh treatment. However, he later realizes that being punished by his mother was better than being slapped by the angry neighbour, whose window he had broken during play. That's because the mother's punishment was controlled; she also loves her child and ensures his safety. On the other hand, the punishment from an angry, non-loving neighbour could have been disproportionate and more painful. Similarly, when a devotee of Krishna suffers, he is monitored by his loving Lord. This knowledge, awareness and feelings of love, known as satcitananda, create a state of deeper happiness—a Home State.

ISKCON invites and captivates millions of people every year with its beautiful temples, grand festivals, splendid deities, melodious kirtans and delightful food festivals—all aimed at helping us discover our Home State. Many Hare Krishna devotees find their Home State through the chanting of God's holy names. I have friends who can spend hours dressing and worshipping the deities. Others find solace in writing journals, seeking respite from the multitude of miseries that relentlessly assail them. Some seek shelter in listening to devotional classes or sitting quietly in the sacred temple premises. While the details may differ, each sincere spiritual practitioner has their Home State—a place where they feel safe and united with the divine Lord. You know you're in your Home State when time becomes irrelevant and you can stay there for hours, experiencing deep fulfilment.

In this state, we can live in the world like our other friends, experiencing both suffering and enjoyment, but with a difference. We have our loving Lord accompanying us in every moment of our lives. By staying true to our authentic selves within our Heart Space, we can contribute more effectively to bringing goodness and love to this planet.

While living true to our real selves in our Heart Space, we can also contribute more effectively to bringing goodness and love to this planet.

There are numerous shining examples of men and women on this planet who, driven by a quiet sense of peace and fearlessness, have added value to the lives of countless others.

Let us now examine one such case study.

# Fearless Contribution: The Essence of Heart Space

*I would rather die a meaningful death than live a meaningless life.*

—Corazino Aquino

Two striking contrasts in the history of the Philippines reveal this principle.

Imelda Marcos and her husband, Ferdinand, pillaged their country, amassing billions of dollars while millions starved. Imelda, a beauty queen, indulged in a lavish lifestyle, collecting thousands of pairs of shoes, priceless gems and living in vanity. Ferdinand, as president, imposed martial law, keeping the country impoverished, the opposition suppressed and the citizens desperate for change.

Benigno Aquino emerged as the leader of the crusade against the Marcos dictatorship, offering hope during their reign of excess. However, upon his return from the USA, he was brazenly murdered at the Manila airport, as witnessed by TV cameras. This tragic event thrust his reticent wife, Corazino (Cory), into the spotlight. The nation rallied behind her, viewing her as the best option to counter the despotic rule of Ferdinand and Imelda Marcos.

Corazino humbly resisted the spotlight, having always considered herself a simple housewife dedicated to raising her five children and supporting her husband. Even during Benigno's rallies, she preferred to cheer him on from the crowd rather than sharing the stage. However, circumstances had dramatically changed. After careful deliberation and sincere prayers, she made the courageous decision to lead the struggle for democracy. Ferdinand called for snap elections, shamelessly rigged the results and declared himself the winner. Cory vehemently opposed him, enduring rumours and demeaning remarks about her gender and capabilities. To weaken her, Ferdinand played a dirty macho card, saying she is, after all, a weak woman whose place is in the bedroom.

Undeterred by the challenges, Corazino Aquino led her people in the world's most successful non-violent uprising against a dictatorial government. Hailed as the 'Mother of Asian Democracy', she became the first female president of the Philippines. With innate humility, Cory acknowledged that leadership was not her calling and refused to stand for re-election after her term expired. Unaffected by power and position, she selflessly donated her wealth to charity, living a life of honour and dignity.

When she passed away in 2009, the world mourned and celebrated her contributions. Throughout her life, she fearlessly faced multiple attempted coups against her government. During one such incident, armed men attacked the President's residence. As her trusted colonel positioned his guards to defend against the enemy, he was astonished by Cory's composed emotional state. Inside the house, he witnessed her calmly combing her hair and walking to safety. Intrigued by her unwavering composure, he asked her how she remained so calm. Serenely, Cory replied that she combed her hair because she needed to appear presentable as the president of her country.

In retrospect, her fearlessness and detachment were born from a sense of service. She had nothing to lose and her sole possession was a deep commitment to making a meaningful contribution to her family and nation.

# Part III

# Chapter 6

# How to Live and Flourish in the Heart Space

## Secrets from the Monastery

### *Ten essays from a monk's daily practice*

'There are many closely guarded secrets even in the renounced order,' said my senior and mentor when I joined the monastic order.

He had already been a monk for over twenty-five years when I joined. Today, I have also spent twenty-five years in our ashram, and I see him blissfully do the same things daily. So, in effect, he has been practising spiritual life for over five decades. He journals, meditates under a banyan tree, worships deities in the temple, cleans the monastery, cooks for the deities and gives love to our community members.

I recall that conversation in December 1998, when I had joined the ashram and asked him for his guidance and blessings. 'Hmm,' he said meditatively, adding, 'the cyclones and tidal waves leave a trail of devastation and no one is spared. Whether you are a monk living in a quaint monastery or struggling outside in the big, bad, mad world, we all face similar demons; after all, the mind doesn't care who you are or where you are. Yet, we all have our own little secrets here that help us battle our internal enemies.'

His toothless smile was a bait that invited me to explore the inner world of the resilient monks. What kept them going for so many years, both gratefully and productively? I wanted to explore the enigma behind my mentor's smile.

Besides, now that I look back, I too have gone through a roller-coaster ride in my inner world. I have seen my inner demons attack me viciously. I have slipped, struggled and risen again under the shelter of my seniors. Living happily and productively in this world that constantly threatens to upset our inner status quo is not easy. To discover our Home State and, more importantly, flourish in that space, requires more than mere academic knowledge of the scriptures. We study sacred books, pray for hours and serve our community, and when we do this daily, we learn and grow. Besides, there are amazing histories, stories and allegories contained in the Upanishads and Puranas that were compiled thousands of years ago. And yet, mysteriously, these wisdom tales speak about our times and challenges.

In the following ten chapters, I share some lessons I have learnt personally and some I have observed from my seniors who have applied the teachings of the ancient texts in their own lives. I can assure you that I have known at least a hundred friends—both living inside and outside the monastery—who today live in an abundant Heart Space.

And what follows now in this book is a tool kit containing four inviolable principles, designed to help you find and flourish in your Heart Space.

## These Four Principles Are:

**The Being State:** the four As, as a prerequisite to enter the Heart Space

**Slowing Down Our Lives by Breathing:** the importance of pause and conscious breath

**The Art of Journalling:** the techniques and benefits of putting your mind on paper

**The Life of Prayer in Bhakti Yoga:** exploring surrender, humility, scriptures and steadily chanting the Holy Names to develop a relationship with God.

\* \* \*

But before all of that, we need some baby steps to enter the Heart Space. We have a unique gift that we need to tap to flourish in the Heart Space. We will study this in the next chapter.

# Chapter 7

# Baby Steps to Enter the Heart Space

*One whose happiness is within, who is active within, who rejoices within and is illumined within, is actually the perfect mystic. He is liberated in the Supreme, and ultimately, he attains the Supreme.*

—Bhagavad Gita (5.24)

If you win one million rupees, you could either waste it away or double with a proper investment.

Right now, the good Lord above has bestowed on you a million-rupee gift.

If I asked you to give me one of your fingers for a thousand rupees, would you give it away? You have ten fingers on your hands and legs. Then you have kidneys, liver, pancreas and other limbs that you dearly value; all of them mean more than a million rupees to you!

## Your Unique Gift

Your body–mind–time (BMT) is your unique gift. The way you use it determines your happiness. How you take care of your BMT reveals if you are in charge of your life or if someone else holds the reins, and are you a mere puppet, a victim of conditions beyond yourself?

If you closely analyse your gifts, you'll realize that you have the ability to think, rationalize, discriminate, take decisions, make choices, inquire and explore a higher dimension of happiness. This is amazing! And it's come to you!

Now, the question we need to ask ourselves is: what am I doing with the BMT given to me? Am I using this gift to make my social life better or am I also using it to make my internal life stronger?

## Our Two Lives: External and Internal

Most of us use BMT for our external lives—the party, office, relationships, money and social media presence.

But do you realize you have another life—an internal life—where you are all alone, with your fears, deep insecurities, concerns and subconscious patterns, which don't go away even if you are busy the whole day.

Travelling from Borivali (a north-western suburb of Mumbai) to Churchgate (south Mumbai) in the local trains of Mumbai, you meet many strangers, packed together in a compartment. You pick up a conversation, maybe argue over recent political situations and then you discuss other issues. At Andheri, some of them get down and new passengers enter. At Dadar, a few more leave you and finally, as you near Churchgate, you realize you were all alone, anyway. You may never meet them again. We meet many 'strangers' in our sojourn in this world—we make relationships, work together, serve and love. One by one, we all part ways, sooner or later, and eventually a realization dawns on each one of us—we are all alone.

In the forest of our inner world, we are alone. When the last part of the dust settles after the caravan passes, you sit all alone on a bench in this lonely forest. A gnawing vacuum stares at you. Are you at peace with yourself? Do you accept yourself the way you are? Do you spend time connecting to your own inner self—do you ask and discover answers to the question of 'Who am I?' or 'What's the purpose of my life?' Or maybe you are too busy to pause and ponder. Your inability to relax and reflect on what's really meaningful to you leads to a disconnect from your inner self, and our busyness simply leads to more pain and suffering. Ironically, we lose control of our lives, although we are busy. We are engaged but lost!

And yet, we needn't be lonely. When we connect to God, we find shelter and can also have effective and meaningful relationships with all the 'strangers' we meet in the train journey of our lives.

How can we use the BMT to enter the Heart Space?

## Empower Yourself

A song from the 1954 award-winning Hindi film *Boot Polish* graphically explains how empowered we are: John, a bootlegger, teaches little children self-respect and asks, '*Nane munne bacche teri mutti mein kya hai?*' (Oh, little children, what's in your fists?)

The children reply, '*Mutti mein hai tagdeer hamari.*' (Our fists contain our destiny.)

A child today may sing, 'My fists contain a smartphone.' And that means you've lost your destiny to someone or something else.

Our two lives—external and internal— are a reality that we can't deny. Inordinate time spent on social media (the external reality) makes our inner lives—the second reality of our lives—a wreck.

We follow rules and etiquette for our external lives. In a social setting, you know how to sit, talk and behave. You've been taught not to dig your nose—that's dirty. 'Don't yawn or burp loudly—that's bad manners.' You sit and speak with grace. You have learnt how to be effective in your social life.

But do you know that you also need to follow rules in your private life—to be effective as you tackle your fears and insecurities? And when surprises and shocks pounce on you, what do you do? How do you maintain inner equilibrium amidst some tragic news, a betrayal or a painful situation?

What percentage of time do you spend in a day taking care of your internal life vis-à-vis your external roles? Fifty–fifty? Or maybe 10 per cent time is for your internal life and 90 per cent for your external life? Is there a healthy balance? Are you equipped or trained to take care of your inner world, which could get scary at times? Years pass by with no seemingly life-altering setbacks, but suddenly a crisis comes and how well you have trained all these years to take care of your emotional world will determine how you pass this sudden exam.

## Making Ourselves Strong Internally

Using the BMT daily, sincerely, for our inner stability is like watering the root of a tree. A huge banyan tree gives shelter to many birds and insects, yet its strength is below the ground.

Cyclones can't uproot the tree because it has strong roots. Calgary Tower in Canada is 191 metres long and 60 per cent of it is below the ground. We may be attracted by a beautiful house and its architecture, but a civil engineer will be interested in knowing how the foundation of the building was laid.

A famous actor lived with chronic back pain for many years. The reason for his suffering? He did sincerely work out, but he worked on the upper portion of his body—that part seen on magazine covers and advertisements. His attractive biceps, chest and shoulders had women drooling, but because he ignored his legs and knees, it caused a debilitating effect on his lower back.

We work on areas that the world recognizes—our Facebook profiles, Instagram posts and, in general, our personalities. In order to get more social mileage, we may ignore the important aspects of our lives, such as our character and emotional well-being. Over time, this prolonged neglect takes a toll—despite the external and verifiable success, a bedevilling emptiness may stare at us. Core spiritual activities like prayer, meditation or journalling can help build our emotional resilience, and the benefits of this initiative are reaped over time, especially during a crisis.

The question that now begs itself is: how do we get strong internally, to be able to enter the Heart Space?

To become strong internally, we need to spend more time in metaphysical reality.

There are three realities in our lives.

## The Ladder of Consciousness—Three Realities

Imagine a ladder whose lowest rung is an illusion. In the middle, we have a temporary reality and at the top of this ladder, there is an endless or eternal reality.

We are preoccupied with some movies or video games—unreal issues—at the bottom of the ladder. We seem to have no time to look beyond Netflix series; although a higher reality beckons us, we are stuck in a lower reality.

The three Es: Electronic reality (virtual reality), Ephemeral (physical) and Eternal (metaphysical) reality—our lives oscillate between these three spheres of existence. We run up and down this ladder, while some of us stay stuck at the lowest rung.

When you see beautiful rain on your smartphone's screen, you may be captivated. You may watch an emotional movie in a theatre. But it's all light flashing on the screen. The rain or the high-octane thriller you watch has no existence at all—it's just not there.

## Electronic or Virtual Reality Is an Illusion

In a movie, when the thunder strikes, the trees whirl and swing and the heroine falls into the arms of the hero. And if you've invested your time as well as your emotions in this, then you've spent time on something that just doesn't exist. It's a mirage—there is no rain or no girl or boy expressing love; it's simply a light flashing on a screen. Yet, it captivates us; some spend many precious hours a day on our electronic gadgets or the digital world. Bewitched by technology, we lose control over our lives. Here's a very sobering quote: 'Technology is a great servant but a terrible master.' Instead of using our smartphones, we are now dependent on them; as a result, these gadgets are using us!

The more time we spend in the virtual world, the more we connect to a reality that simply doesn't exist.

I heard a nice quote in one class that captures our predicament well: 'We are living at a time when capturing moments using our phones is more important than actually living those moments with whoever is beside us.'

That which doesn't exist is called 'Maya' in Vedic parlance. And wisdom books from the East refer to our attachments to non-real phenomena as Maya. When a person suffers but imagines it to be enjoyment—like a camel relishing its own blood while sucking thorns—it's called Maya.

When we are bored and stare at our phone screens or fidget without any particular reason, we are in Maya—illusion.

Now is the time to rise above on this ladder.

At the lowest rung of the ladder of consciousness, there is Maya—an illusion or attachment to an unreal existence. We have named it 'Electronic Reality'.

## Physical or Ephemeral Reality

The second level—the middle rung of the ladder—is the ephemeral or temporary reality, which refers to all our daily activities. We go to the office, spend time with our loved ones, exercise or eat food to take care of our bodies. But our jobs, relationships and health—the body itself—will be wiped out of existence by time. Everything is temporary in this world, but most people have their energy, emotions and time deeply invested in the fleeting issues of this temporary world. We love, fight, fret and fume, desire, hate and worry endlessly about issues that are like a water bubble on a lotus leaf—it's gone and over.

Traditionally, our attachment to this fleeting world was called Maya. But Maya's more sinister form in recent times is the electronic or virtual world. So together, both rungs are an illusion, but still, we can use existence at both layers for connecting to God and contributing to society. We could use our smartphones to serve others and to listen to devotional songs or watch spiritual discourses. Likewise, our life at the middle rung, with family and work, can be used for a noble cause—loving service and helping others to connect to God.

## Moving from Illusion to Eternity

The third level—the topmost rung of the ladder of consciousness—is eternal reality. Eternal is something that remains—it doesn't fade away with time. It is an endless space—the topmost rung of the ladder of consciousness.

When you spend time by the ocean, on a mountain or at an ancient temple, you feel a certain peace in your heart. Although even mountains and oceans are temporary phenomena on this planet, relatively speaking, in comparison to our brief lives, they seem to have been there forever. And there is something within us that is also eternal—it doesn't die when the body perishes. That 'soul' or 'force' finds shelter when you sit under a huge banyan tree or when you stare up at the full moon in a starlit sky. Something has been around for a really long time in this world, and when we connect to that, we find peace. That serenity emerges from the space of Brahman—the eternal reality of our lives.

Compare the experience of watching the rain on an electronic screen to a beautiful rain shower outside your window. Or contrast the smell of a high-end, popular brand perfume with the natural fragrance of a rose flower or the smell of earth mixed with rainwater. If you are mindful, you'll notice a dog on the street entertains you more than a movie's most thrilling special effects. But many people today are trapped by their smartphones and the visuals they offer. As someone wisely said, 'I finally realized it . . . People are prisoners of their phones. That's why they are called "cell" phones.'[5]

The more we move up the ladder—from the electronic world to the eternal sphere of existence—we'll find the transition from a stimulating life to a satisfying life.

Spending some time daily in the eternal sphere—like chanting mantras, worshipping the Lord or hearing classes—

helps us connect to our eternal existence. The strength we derive from a life at the top rung helps us navigate our lives more effectively at the lower rung.

On days when I spend quality time in prayer and meditation, I notice that I am able to use my smartphone more judiciously. And at the middle rung, I am able to empathize and serve my family and friends more responsibly.

Therefore, the key to an effective life is to make our inner life strong, and in order to make our internal life solid, we need to spend time daily in prayer and meditation.

## Belonging to God (Metaphysical or Eternal Reality)

In our inner world, we have a natural attraction to 'belong'. We want to feel 'safe' and 'sheltered'—at home. This is commonly understood as peace.

Just as a young boy and girl get attracted to each other, there seems to be no logic behind it; it just happens. They fall in love just like that! Likewise, in our internal world, it's natural for us to find peace and shelter. It's innate to belong to someone or something higher than our own selves.

Just as a child feels safe in the arms of her mother, when we grow up, we look for that same experience through varied pursuits, possessions or relationships. Yet a troubling void stares at us. We never seem to be totally satisfied. That's because we are seeking peace in things outside of us.

If we make the search inward, a little effort can help us fall in love with a higher sense of self—known differently in various traditions. In Vedic culture this is called atman and there are even higher levels, known as paramatma and Bhagavan or Krishna.

But guess what? Somebody comes in the way! And it's you! Our lives are full of ourselves—our fleeting daily worries about house, finances and relationships make it extremely difficult for us to go inward to an eternal reality. If you keep a ten-rupee coin close to your eyes, it can block your vision of the sun. But how many quadrillion times bigger is the sun compared to a small coin? Our 'ten-rupee' issues could blind us to the beautiful reality of the 'sun' like God, universal goodness or a deep sense of peace that's abundantly available, and it's eternal and free!

Yet, it all seems so distant and vague because the ten-rupee issue engulfs our consciousness. If we can spend a few minutes daily disidentifying ourselves from all our material designations, we'd 'fall in love' with this higher, spiritual reality, and it would happen naturally and soon.

## The Baby Steps—Learn to Be Present

Pranay, an old friend of mine, once showed me his old family photographs—his grandfather and great-grandfather and their siblings graced the frame. As he pointed to one of the elderly men, he shared how this man had won an award from the British government and the impact it had on civil society around 150 years ago. As we conversed and skimmed through his various collections, he abruptly stopped and said, 'I realize it's all about my family and I've been babbling on for such a long time. But I see you are so present and happy to hear all this.' He seemed surprised at my interest in a family that might mean nothing to me.

I told him I was relishing this discussion because I was not simply seeing his great-grandparents. I was trying to enter the Mumbai space of 150 years ago—the day and times when the British crown ruled our country. 'Your narration of your ancestors is connecting me to people and places who had their own stories and challenges', I said, adding, 'but the people you speak about are all like us; there's something common between them, who lived 100 years ago, and us struggling in the twenty-first century. I am seeing oneness here.' The legendary Roman emperor Marcus Aurelius said, 'What we do in life, echoes in eternity.'

This is the key to entering an eternal space: choose a time and event, and when you are there, just be present and let go of the mental resistance to judge. As I heard about his great family, I decided this was my time to find peace, shelter and my Home State. I wasn't comparing or analysing his family; I was simply basking in the presence of the sound, of what he spoke. We need to let go of our mental world, release our biases and prejudices when we hear or see and receive the eternity that speaks to us.

Another friend of mine, Rajat, sent me videos made in the early 1920s of cities and parks where people walked, children played and life seemed to go on as nonchalantly as it happens today. I was present and watching each child and tree in the blurred video with attention. At a certain point, there were ninety-five-year-old men and women being interviewed, and they spoke about their childhood and their grandparents. Basically, I was listening to the life and culture of humans living in the 1750s! I had goosebumps. Those men and women lived on the same earth that we traverse now. They breathed the same air and drank the same water, and they laughed, cried, rejoiced and left us—all on the same planet. Something has surely remained here over these centuries, and even before that. We too shall die soon, and 300 years later, our descendants will embark on their own journey. Yet all of us from the past and present are connected to the future; there is eternity inviting us for a connection. We are all connected.

A few moments daily in this space of oneness help one enter the space of shelter. We realize our insignificance in this giant cosmos, and paradoxically, we also feel safe and loved.

One of my earliest spiritual experiences was while studying in my college library. One day, I was engrossed reading a book, *My Thirty Years in India* by Edmund Cox. He speaks about the lives and struggles of Indians, and his job as an inspector of police in the 1850s.[6] His detailed descriptions of how Indians lived and celebrated life in the nineteenth century were engrossing. And I was fully present, reading. Suddenly, at a certain point, I felt an overwhelming sense of love surge from my heart—I knew instantly, in a sense of knowing beyond what we normally think is knowing, that I was one with the universe. Africans, Americans, Muslims and men and women of the past—and this entire world, in fact, the universe is one family and we are all connected to each other. I knew I was 'Home'—in a state of shelter. It didn't matter then whether I lived or died. I was undying, eternal and seemed to live forever—I belonged to a reality greater than the library I was sitting in. I knew at that moment that I was not confined to this body, my home or the city. I had entered another dimension of existence—an eternal sphere.

To enter a space of eternity, you choose a time and place and then be present. Throw away the clock and allow yourself to be directed by a force beyond you.

But if you choose to be present while drinking liquor or watching a movie, you are connected to a life-alienating reality. A movie is simply a light flashing on a screen and liquor lowers your consciousness. We need to choose an activity or a state of being that helps us rise to a higher version of ourselves and not degrade to more bonding with the temporary or unreal.

## Chanting and Studying Books of Wisdom

Chanting the Holy Names or reading books of wisdom—the same names that the sages have chanted over millennia and the scriptures that are read over thousands of years—carry the energy of eternity. When we are present chanting and reading, we go beyond the letters or the sound, and we enter the space of what they represent.

God, or Krishna, is a reality and we find His love and a sense of belongingness with Him as we render submissive, aural reception to His Names.

Srila Prabhupada was leaving San Francisco to go to India and his students felt sad at the imminent separation. 'You chant Hare Krishna here and I'll chant Hare Krishna in India', Srila Prabhupada said, 'and although we are separated by ten thousand miles, we'll be bound together by the Holy Names.'

Through chanting and reading scriptures, Srila Prabhupada found a connection to his predecessor teachers and to Lord Chaitanya Mahaprabhu, who appeared 550 years ago. Srila Prabhupada implored his students to spend quality time daily in this space of 'eternity' to connect to our undying souls and the eternal Lord.

## Two Rules to Enter the Heart Space

Our relationship with Krishna is eternal and Krishna is inviting us to explore this relationship with Him.

As we learn to be more mindful, we enter the being state—the state that catapults a seeker to the Heart Space.

Before we enter the being state, we need to remember two important rules to enter an eternal space: first, we need to give up stimulation for the sake of satisfaction. And secondly, we need a 'basket of activities'—a set of actions that truly define us.

## Rule 1: Regulate Stimulation

Practically speaking, this means we need to be willing to embrace the pain of boredom.

When we joined the monastery, we'd sit for hours during our meditation sessions and during the marathon four- to five-hour classes. If we got bored, we'd bear with our minds and gently come back to hearing the class. However, nowadays, if we are bored, we are just a couple of seconds away from getting stimulated—we have the smartphone to distract us. Boredom is seen as our enemy. The truth is, when we are bored, if we avoid stimulation, we'd find an amazing sense of peace. Creativity takes birth in stillness and peace. The dopamine drive only exhausts us and prevents us from experiencing the present moment.

We will study this phenomenon in greater detail later in the next chapter, where we will see the power of acceptance and allowing (the four As) to enter a 'being' state.

## Rule 2: The 'Basket of Activity' in the Mind

Kevin Carter's photographs shook the world. In particular, one image of a hungry Sudanese child collapsed on the ground while a vulture eyed the boy nearby suggested a scary possibility: did the scavenger feast on the flesh of the dying child? The picture first appeared in *New York Times* and was soon on the front page of almost every daily newspaper in the world. The horrified readers asked uncomfortable questions about the ethics and morality of it all. Carter, a South African photojournalist, had churned human emotions. While accolades came his way, many, like *St Petersburg Times*, criticized him: 'The man adjusting his lens . . . another vulture on the scene!'

Carter cried; his mind plunged in guilt.

He won the Pulitzer Prize in 1993. Three months later, he committed suicide.

On that fateful afternoon, when he took the iconic photograph, he drove the vulture away. Besides, he took risks travelling in the famine and civil war-infested zone. Although he worked hard and had even become a hero of sorts, he was depressed; the haunting memories of corpses, killings and suffering took a toll on his heart.

For many of us, it's the opposite of what Carter faced. He did his job well, but a flood of negativity all around him overwhelmed him and he found little or no cause for joy. We, on the other hand, may have enough reasons to celebrate. Still, just one sullen thought could drown us in sorrow for the rest of the day.

## The Mind's Stubbornness

The mind has an inexhaustible appetite to feast upon negative experiences. From an excess of happy events, it expertly picks up one unpleasant incident and chews it with the gusto of a teenager's fetish for bubblegum. When the juice gets sucked out of the gum, the boy may inflate a bubble to wile his time away. Similarly, the devil within finds syrup in grumbling over a failure; or a perceived injustice by the boss could abruptly throw you into an angry mode. Soon, however, the fluid is out of the event; the mind then swells it and blows it far beyond proportion.

What'd happen if the teenager puffs their bubble beyond a certain size? It would explode and fall on their face. They would then clumsily pick up each strand of the stuck gum. If we don't check the mind's fizz, that's often cut off from reality, it would likewise get stuck on our consciousness and it's not as easy to disentangle the scattered filaments from our psyche.

Recently a leading publisher rejected my book proposal on a day that also saw me achieve many of my self-growth goals. I exercised, read scriptures, gave two talks, wrote an hour, improved relationships with friends, learned poems and much more. Still, the mind moaned: 'Oh, I am unworthy. This publisher is selfish and business minded. They are opportunistic . . .'

Pessimistic self-talk often goes unnoticed by our higher awareness; we don't realize its sinister presence in our inner world. It's time we wake up to the mind's deathly gallows— it's deadly, the threat is real and, before you realize it, you'll plunge into a quicksand.

## The 'Basket' of Happy Activities

Therefore, it's critical for our well-being that we carry a 'basket' of happy activities in our minds.

Spend some solitary moments and write down what defines you—who are you? Then you could list things that help you live an authentic life. These 'things to do' are the items in your basket.

When you are bored or feeling low, look at your basket, pick any one of the things and make yourself cheerful. The secret to saving yourself from repeated letdowns by the mind is to have a lot of meaningful things to do. The choice gives you variety as well and helps circumvent the mind's repeated tantrums.

For those lost in anxious thoughts, contentment lies covered like fire in dry grass. An active life is a spark that could set your joy ablaze. It's not enough to analyse the mind in the head; it's time we got our body—hands and legs—moving to stay happy. And when you are not thinking but instead doing things, especially the ones that you love to do, you enter what the psychologists call the 'flow'—a state of absorption where you transcend the sense of space and time.

## Avoid the 'Should' and 'Should Not' Language

When a friend in our monastery tried the basket exercise, he wrote a lot of things that came to his heart. But then he also scratched off some items from the list.

I probed him about why he did that.

'But I am a monk; how can I desire to drench and dance in the rain?'

'Do you want to do it?' I asked again.

'That's not important', he reiterated, 'we are monks and can't cross our boundaries.'

I humbly suggested, 'My dear friend, what you can't do or what's permitted for you is the second step. First, please write down what you want, regardless of whether it's feasible.'

I explained that once we have the list ready, we can slowly explore the challenges of fulfilling them within the constraints we have chosen to impose on ourselves.

It's essential that you don't let the rules of the world throttle your imagination. You may be delighted by the possibilities.

Akash, my college friend, had a weakness for sweets. I didn't see any harm in it until it began to take a toll on his body and mind. He grabbed a bar of chocolate whenever he was stressed and that was many times during the day. Although munching cinnamon buns and sucking ice cream lollies elevated his mood, the calories, fat, sugar and caffeine worried him. His fear of developing Type 2 diabetes added to his pain; he felt sadder and desperately sought relief. That's when he grabbed chocolate again, indulging in the very act that he attempted to overcome. The more he tried disentangling the Gordian knot tied by his mind, he felt sucked into quicksand and went further away from his purpose.

The 'basket' was the panacea—a healthy alternative that he needed.

One day, he compiled a list of activities that defined him—things that helped him connect deeper to himself and contribute to others' happiness. In a symbolic basket, he piled up these activities. From experience, he knew he couldn't trust his mind, so he put the basket outside as well. He drew a picnic bag on an A-4 size paper and using creative images, wrote down the following: jogging, reading novels, listening to flute music (Hindustani classical), journalling, cycling, yoga, etc.

Daily indulgence of the good acts kept him in excellent spirits and his mind was nurtured. Over time, living in a satisfying space helped improve his awareness; he now catches his slipping mind faster. And the familiarity with his arsenal gives him confidence to take prompt action.

## Winning the Mind Game

It's the words of St Francis (of Assisi) that first hinted at the basket, 'Start by doing what's necessary; then do what's possible, and suddenly you are doing the impossible.'

The basket is our repertoire against the mind's relentless attack. Whenever you feel terrible, look at your container and pick up anyone from the list.

In time, a realization dawned on Akash—he had earlier grabbed chocolate because it fulfilled his need for excitement. Now, the healthy options in his basket attacked his boredom with a satisfying experience. He now has an innocuous-looking 'basket' that's helping him win the mind game, albeit slowly. To create the basket, he needed to know who he was, but now the basket's helping him know what he could be.

Often, like Akash, we recognize what's not healthy for us, yet we succumb to those very things. But the 'basket' brings hope. The American author Robert Kiyosaki rightly said, 'Don't let the fear of losing be greater than the excitement of winning.'

\* \* \*

*Once we are doing that which helps us connect to ourselves and we also perform those actions mindfully, tolerating the need of the mind to get stimulated, then we slowly move from 'doing' to 'being'.* The next chapter explains the phenomenon of 'Being' in greater detail.

# Chapter 8

# The Being State: From Human 'Doing' to Human 'Being'

*For one who is a neophyte in the yoga system, work is said to be the means; and for one who is already elevated in yoga, cessation of all material activities is said to be the means.*
—Bhagavad Gita (6.3)

'Do I have to wait to die and go back to the kingdom of God to realize God? Or does He come here as well?' asked a student after my weekly Bhagavad Gita class.

'You can experience God NOW!' I said, quite animatedly. 'You go to Him after death only if you receive Him while you are living in this world.'

'What do I do to receive Him now?' he probed me further.

I sensed he was in the 'struggle' house at this moment. I sought to pull him into the 'surrender' zone—the Heart Space.

'Well, you don't "do" anything; you just "be"' I said, and added, 'Congratulations—you are in the Heart Space now!'

He looked at me, puzzled. 'I see you guys do a lot of rituals, prayers and temple worship. Why "do" all of that if you just have to "be"?'

## Two Steps to Experience God

'There are two steps to experiencing God in this world,' I slowly gave clarification. 'First, you "do" activities that help you connect with God. These rituals are initially a means to pull you out of the world of "sense gratification" or illusion; they place you on the runway to God. But often our mind pulls us out of the spiritual path, and therefore we need to "struggle" or "do" these activities diligently. If you are a Bhakti Yoga practitioner, you chant, pray, read scriptures, serve, etc. Each tradition has its own discipline and methods that are designed to help us come to awareness/God/Krishna/universal consciousness. But when "struggle" or "doing" the rituals is predominant in your consciousness, it's time to let go and "surrender" or "be". And that's the second step. Just abandon the struggle and be present in the Bhakti Yoga activities.'

'Hmm,' he jiggled his head slowly and remained silent. I knew he was processing what I had just said.

After a few seconds, he replied, 'But it seems impossible not to struggle. For any healthy experience, I need to struggle, whereas if I had to invoke my lower nature, there are abundant alternatives. I could just "be" while watching Netflix or while smoking or drinking. But why do I "do" and struggle when I chant or pray?'

Now, it was my turn to wiggle my head and I sat silently. My thoughts raced to all my 'struggles' in spiritual practices. For many years, my 'experiences' were overshadowed by my zealous pursuits of the various practices in our tradition.

A few seconds later, I took a long breath, smiled and concurred with his concerns.

What followed next was a candid discussion and we zeroed in on the principle of Awareness–Acceptance–Allow that helps us live and flourish in the Heart Space—moving from 'do' to 'be' and letting go of the 'struggle.'

## The Psychology of 'Doing' and 'Being'

When you get things done, you are 'doing'. It could be cooking a meal, planning a holiday, sending a satellite to space or trying to be happy.

When you have cooked a meal, you have plugged a gap. When you finalized a holiday plan, you have completed a task and when you finish a project or a journey, you have successfully 'done'.

The 'doing' is necessary for leading an effective life. But there are some areas where doing doesn't work.

When you relax, you don't 'do'; you 'be'. You let go of the urge to 'do'. In contrast to 'doing', a state of 'being' is when you allow things to happen to you. While relaxing by the ocean, you let the gentle breeze caress you. You hear the soft rumbling of the waves and see the vast expanse of water. Your mind wanders and slowly comes back to the present. You are not on a project to complete anything. You are not trying to achieve any particular level of meditation. You just 'be'.

This is the 'task negative' mode of the brain—a state that not only nourishes our brain but also is our default setting. On the other hand, the 'task positive' mode of the brain is when you 'do' and focus on your goals. You are concentration personified, as you think, write and do what you are supposed to do. But you need to balance the 'task positive' with the 'task negative'; the 'doing' with the 'being'.

When you go on a morning walk with no particular thing to achieve or do and you simply walk with abandon, you access a space beyond 'struggle'. Many Nobel laureates have shared that some of their most amazing ideas that manifested in their heads happened when they weren't particularly thinking about it! They were in a relaxed state and the juxtaposition of various thoughts in their heads happened. You misplace your umbrella and frantically search for it, wondering where you kept it. Unsuccessful, you let go and carry on with other duties. Suddenly, out of nowhere, you remember where you had kept the umbrella. What just happened? You let go of the 'doing' mode of the brain and things were revealed to you, just like that.

The psychology of 'being' is detachment and the state of 'doing' is control.

We need control in life, but a control freak is unhappy and in disorder. Therefore, we also need to practise detachment and 'let go'.

The best way to gain balance and control of our inner state is to let go at the right time and allow ourselves to be an instrument in the hands of higher forces. This is the state of 'being' that awards rich benefits.

## The 'Doing' Addict

Near our monastery, we have a beautiful garden called the Hanging Garden. Sometimes, I would go there for a stroll in the evenings. As the services and hectic schedule of the monastery kept me busy, I'd look at the watch and calculate the hours remaining until I could go to the garden and relax. I'd anticipate the walk around fragrant rose bushes and I'd imagine sitting under the large banyan tree. This hope of a well-spent evening helped me tolerate monotonous meetings during the day. But over time, I realized my precious time in the garden wasn't as fulfilling as I had imagined. I wondered what had gone wrong. One day, exhausted after many meetings and classes, I consciously chose to breathe and relax. As my mind wandered into plan-making, I slowly came back to relax and appreciate the beauty of the garden. My mind slowed down and I let go of the itch to look at my watch. I sat 'doing nothing'—in a state of 'being'. Eureka! Just then, a realization dawned on me that during the last few weeks, my time in the garden was beset with plan-making and problem-solving in my head. Externally, I was in the serene garden, but my mind was 'doing' many things. And that was because I was in the 'doing' mode the whole day and when I reached the garden, the hangover of the day's mental patterns remained. I had become a 'doing' addict. At this moment, it became crystal clear to me why the garden wasn't an exciting proposition anymore.

Soon, the mind attempted to fix this lacuna. This was yet another 'doing'—I wanted to sort out a plan that would help me come to a relaxed state. I didn't realize then that I simply had to let go of the plan-making and I'd be happy. But as addicted I was to 'doing', I wouldn't let go till I had figured out a plan that would help me 'be' relaxed. Ironically, it was the plan to relax that was my scourge and that prevented me from relaxing! My determination and resolve to relax were the very bane of my existence. I was unable to relax because I thought too much about relaxing. I was 'doing' instead of simply 'being'.

The more I struggled to relax, the more elusive it was. My mind was speeding, like the exhaust fan in our bathroom.

The solution was simple: just let go of the plan and relax.

How do I let go? How do I 'be'?

## AWARENESS, ACCEPTANCE, ALLOW and Don't ACT—the Four As of the Being Cycle

Let this be a five-minute exercise to 'be'. The first step is that you resolve to simply observe the mind (Awareness) and not 'do' anything the mind urges you to do. If you rise and act in this 'be' period, you've failed the process.

You begin by answering a question: 'What's happening at this moment?'

The answer to this question is Awareness—the first A.

For example, right now, it's raining outside and I see a senior monk strolling in the hallway. If I note this scene as a video camera would pick it up, I have successfully become aware. I could take my awareness to the next level if I could ask the same question about my inner world: 'What's happening in my mind at this moment?'

Your mind could be planning the evening or your mind could express fear at the consequences of today's meeting. The mind would run to a thousand events and if at this moment you know where your mind is, you have practised awareness.

The challenge begins when you begin the journey to second A—Acceptance.

When you pause and become aware of your mind's situation, you may realize you were worrying about your finances. Now, could you 'accept' that you were worrying? This isn't as easy as it seems.

Recently, a friend expressed frustration at his home situation. During the conversation, he feared judgement and immediately clarified, 'Actually, I am not frustrated; it's just that I am struggling a lot.' I listened to him attentively and again, I saw he was pensive. 'Honestly, it's not a struggle', he said sheepishly, 'it's just that I am trying my best to balance my situation at home.' I empathized with him, but knew he had awareness of his predicaments, but he couldn't accept that he was frustrated.

A family sincerely served the oldest member—a bedridden nonagenarian—for over fifteen years until he died. A month later, the couple visited me and expressed regret that they hadn't served their father sincerely. I reassured them that they were exemplary and had done their best for more than a decade. During this period, I was aware it hadn't been easy for the family. In a small house with a tantrum-throwing old man, the family struggled to keep their sanity. I gave them love and comfort. Still, they seemed to be in pain. As our conversation progressed, I asked, 'Are you feeling guilty because you feel a sense of relief after your father died—you are relieved from the hectic and demanding schedule of caring for him? And you are miserable because you feel relief!'

I saw them look at me with stunned expressions. The lady's lower jaw dropped, they exchanged glances, and gave out a long sigh. Tears filled their eyes and they silently affirmed what I had suggested.

I had just helped them move from Awareness to Acceptance. When you feel envious of someone, can you pause, become aware and, most importantly, could you accept your inner state without judging yourself for it?

While awareness is easy—it just requires one to pause and ask what's happening now—acceptance is more difficult. Most people impulsively attempt to change their inner states. Either they declare all's well or pronounce an affirmation that they've overcome all their insecurities. In their desperate attempt to improve their mental condition, they bypass this critical second step—just accept that you are worrying! Or if you are feeling lonely and sad, and you are aware of your melancholy state, can you accept it? We may mechanically say, 'I accept I am feeling lonely.' But this isn't real acceptance and the proof lies in the fact that you are desperate to change your inner state.

You practise acceptance when you don't immediately jump to remove your loneliness; you aren't desperate or in a hurry to overcome your sadness. Your actions aren't an impulsive attempt to change your inner state. Most positive thinking mantras, pep talks and motivational videos on YouTube deny our inherent humanness in being melancholy—it's usually a desperate attempt to become happy.

Acceptance is the ability to tell the mind, 'I am aware that I am sad and I accept this sadness. It's okay to be sad. I wish I was happier, but still, this is what it is—I am miserable and I accept my situation.' There is no analysis or justification for the inner state of mind. You are aware and you accept your situation. Period.

Acceptance punctures the mind's rant. The mind loves to hover on extremes—first it will complain about your finances. Then it would jump to a solution. First it will moan and wail—remain sad. Then it would cry, saying that it's always sad! In the process, you get exhausted by the mind's restless nature. Therefore, before you figure out a solution to the problem imagined by the mind, you need to simply accept your situation—the worry of finances or the grip of melancholy. You may not be happy with your situation, but you need to accept it.

The third A—the step of Allow—is a game changer. After you accept, the mind's rant doesn't stop. So now you allow the worry to remain inside you. You say, 'I now allow this melancholy to stay within me.' When you 'allow', you are giving space to the mind to moan. You are making peace with your first spouse—the mind—and allowing him or her to live in pain. It's a deeper acceptance. You are embracing the discomfort. You now seek to be comfortable with the uncomfortable. You allow your mind to remain sad. This is when you are declaring to the mind that you don't judge it and that you accept your mind for what it is. This is non-judgemental acceptance in practice.

Awareness is knowing that the mind is miserable. Acceptance means to not deny the misery and live with it. Allowing means consciously, without judgement, making peace with your misery.

It's important to clarify that allowing your mind to be in an undesirable state doesn't mean you have capitulated. You still don't like your situation, yet by allowing your mind to remain sad, you are declaring to the universe that you are at peace—in a state of 'being'—and you are not 'doing' anything radical to change your situation. Moreover, this is a powerful declaration that you are not your mind—you have 'accepted' and 'allowed' your mind to be where it is, but you are a different person than your mind.

The paradox of 'being' at peace is that while it appears you have forsaken control, you actually gain more control of your situation. The Navy Seals in the US and the MARCOS (Marine Commandos) in India have an interesting training session called the 'hell week'. It's literally a hell where the participants go through 140 hours of training with barely two hours of rest in a day for one week. The programme is designed to break the soldiers; it's said that a 'hell week' reduces five years from a person's life. And yet there are a few men who have completed two or three 'hell weeks' in their lives. The secret of those who pass this rigorous training programme is that they don't count how many hours remain until the training is over. Those who calculate the number of hours they have spent and how much more they need to tolerate usually fail the test. They can't sustain it till the end. But those who accept their hellish condition and allow the mind's suffering condition to coexist as they pull along with the rigours of the week make it. They pass the gruelling training programme. The secret is that they get more control, although apparently they are allowing their mind to remain in pain.

When you are in emotional pain, if you learn to quietly tolerate it, you are basically embracing it. And when you embrace the pain, you find a strange kind of peace engulfing your heart. Just as the eye of the storm has peace, similarly, when we learn to live with the mind's incessant wails, we discover an ineffable peace.

But the fourth A—Don't Act—is the most important step.

## Applying the Four As—Don't 'DO' Is Key to the 'Being' State

One day, I sat on the terrace of the ashram, relaxing. A friend came by and asked what I was doing. Nonchalantly, I said I was doing nothing. 'You must be planning a class or praying, isn't it?' he probed me; he was incredulous that a 'successful' and 'busy' teacher like myself could be doing nothing. I reassured him that I was indeed doing nothing and that nothing actually meant nothing! 'You are surely memorizing some Sanskrit verses,' he said, again with a nervous smile. When I reassured him again, I added a line that left him confused and shocked: 'You are unable to accept that I am doing nothing because, my dear young man, you need to really work hard to do nothing!'

In a world where busyness and doing are glorified, it's not easy to say you do nothing. When we simply sit with ourselves and relax in a waking state, we are tapping into the power of being alone. When we do nothing in a state of relaxation, creative juices flow and our brain gets some much-needed rest. As the mind wanders everywhere, you gently bring it back to awareness.

## A Case Study

Shyam, a forty-five-year-old friend, was diagnosed with diabetes and advised to abstain from eating sweets. His craving got intense when his wife and children policed his consumption of chocolate. He became desperate and felt miserable.

He tried the three As method to cope with the pain of giving up sweets.

He began with Awareness. His daily practices helped him become aware when his mind craved for sweets (we will learn about improving awareness in the next chapter). It was no longer mindless, impulsive grabbing of sweets. He now had awareness of the pull his mind had on him. However, his determined efforts to restrain eating sweets not only exhausted him mentally but also eventually weakened his resolve. He landed up eating a mouthful of sugar and grabbed sweets indiscriminately after a few days of restrictions. That's when he realized that simply being aware is not sufficient and a determined effort to control the diet is unsustainable.

He now practised the second A (Acceptance). He accepted he had this urge and told himself, 'I accept that I love sweets and I accept the pain I feel now at not having sweets.'

Remember, the key here is not doing anything but simply accepting. His mind immediately roared, 'I accept that I am addicted to sweets and that's okay, so let me grab a chocolate now!'

Instead of acting on this new instinct to grab a chocolate, he again 'accepted' that his mind wants to grab a sweet right now. At this time, he began to 'Allow' the craving to coexist in his mind. 'I give permission for this desire to stay in my mind and I accept the pain of not having the sweets.' As he affirmed this repeatedly, each time investing emotions in it, he could see a sense of peace enter his consciousness, although paradoxically, the pain remained. Again, the mind pulled him in all directions—to pick up his phone and distract himself from the sweets. But this time, he again practised Awareness–Acceptance–Allow by saying, 'I am now aware that the mind wants to pick up the phone to forget the pain of no sweets. I accept this pulling of the mind to check my WhatsApp and I allow this urge to remain in me.'

Notice here that Shyam is accepting and allowing at every moment and not acting. 'Watch the cricket highlights on YouTube', his mind now demanded another distraction from the pain. This time Shyam said to himself, 'I accept that my mind wants to watch cricket and I allow this desire to remain in me.' With each new proposal from the mind to distract him from the pain of not having sweets, Shyam came back to the pain. He faced it upfront, rather than ignoring or denying it.

Often, we are unable to enter the Heart Space because we can't sustain the 'being' state and that happens because we are hardwired to believe that we need to 'do' many things or at least 'this one thing' to be happy. The mind's 'doing' pattern was punctured by Shyam with repeated Awareness–Acceptance–Allow. Until, finally, the mind slowed down and he could transcend the craving. Initially, he sat with the pain of no sweets for half an hour and, through repeated practice over two months, enjoyed a life of no sweets.

Instead of resolving and fixing the problem now, Shyam practised the more effective method of allowing the pain to stay. He had embraced the pain of not having sweets.

Sounds too good to be true? What's the psychological game happening here?

Your partner is in pain. When they vent their frustrations, you could make the bad choice of suggesting 'expert' solutions. Instead, try to listen, understand and silently affirm their goodness—accept your partner for who they are and give them the space to exist with all their pain. The relief they experience when you don't judge them is immense. After the release of their pain, you have someone who is at peace. And they will likely understand you as well. Likewise, when the mind screams and you don't jump to action (which is like giving solutions to your spouse), you are giving permission and space to your mind to be who it is—an incorrigible, restless cry baby. After some time, the mind pauses and you can move on slowly and graciously to your other intended actions for the day. The mind would then likely cooperate, as you have given the mind a space in your existence. After all, you need the mind to achieve your goals.

Let's say instead of this approach, you decide to 'do' things and distract yourself with your smartphone or social media to forget the pain. There is immediate relief, but the problem has compounded and soon enough, the craving will return with vengeance. You can't suppress your desires artificially; you need to face them and have the courage to accept your fallibility.

One may argue that the four As are also a state of 'doing.' Yes, but there is a difference.

It's like removing a thorn from your foot with the help of another thorn, but eventually you throw both of them out. The four As seamlessly disintegrate as you develop more awareness and internalize acceptance.

Spiritual practices may externally appear to be rigorous forms of 'doing', yet there is more to them.

## Spiritual Practices for 'Being'

We perform spiritual practices—'do' with a sense of discipline and eventually learn to enter a space of 'being'. Initially, the practices are a means, and, over time, they become an end in themselves.

As part of our tradition, we chant *Hare Krishna* on our beads. Some of us may consider chanting as a 'means' for some wonderful 'end'. We imagine some spiritual happiness waiting to unfold if we kept chanting the Holy Names of Krishna. However, scriptures explain that over time, we'll realize that the happiness from chanting Hare Krishna is the chanting itself!

An Indian folk tale illustrates this principle nicely:

*A poor old man approached a king and said he had never seen gold in his life and desired to see the king's treasury before he died. Taking pity on him, the king asked his minister to show the gold treasury to the poor man. As the man accompanied the minister through the corridors of the royal palace, he was awestruck by the grandeur and his heart raced in anticipation to see gold. Finally, when he came to the treasury room and saw the gold coins lying in abundance, he was joyful, yet he looked surprised. The minister asked him what the matter was. The man smiled and said he now realizes that the gold that lies in abundance here is the same that he had seen fill up the pillars, chandeliers and the stairs that he walked through to arrive at the treasury. It was gold all the way until he finally came and saw the gold coins!*

Spiritual practitioners experience a similar epiphany after years of sincere practice. Initially, we chant Hare Krishna because we imagine we'll experience some exotic, abstract state of happiness. But, over time, it's chanting that gives a devotee happiness! Theoretically, we know that chanting the Holy Names of the Lord is a spiritual practice but only after sincere and disciplined approach to the practice do we really begin to experience the chanting as a spiritual powerhouse. When Srila Prabhupada was asked in an interview what he hoped to gain from chanting Hare Krishna, he replied, 'By chanting Hare Krishna, we seek to chant more!'

Srila Prabhupada also emphasized that the process of spiritual discipline is not to add something new to our lives. It's essentially to uncover what's already lying hidden beneath the layers of our mind–intelligence–ego. Once, on a morning walk, Srila Prabhupada went to the lake nearby and began to hit the icy water with his walking stick. Seeing the ice break and the crystal clear water appear visible to the devotees, Srila Prabhupada smiled and said, 'This is my job! I break through the artificial layers of our consciousness and help one realize his natural position. We are servants of God and presently, we have many artificial impositions on our minds. As we chant Hare Krishna, these ego-induced identities peel off and we discover our natural, original self as a pure, part and parcel of God.'

## The 'HOW to do it?' Trap—Paralysis by Analysis

A poem of the 1870s called 'The Centipede's Dilemma' attributed to Katherine Craster, lent its name to an effect in psychology called the Centipede Syndrome.

A centipede was happy—quite!
Until a toad in fun
Said, 'Pray, which leg moves after which?'
This raised her doubts to such a pitch,
She fell exhausted in the ditch
Not knowing how to run.[7]

The centipede effect occurs when a normal, unconscious activity gets unsettled by getting conscious of it. A cricket batsman, for example, could overthink how he'd hold the bat, only to find himself unable to play well. Or if you are thinking too much about how you'd knot your tie, you may find your simple task difficult.

When it comes to your mind and spiritual practices, are you like the centipede that got disorganized and couldn't walk after the toad asked her, 'What's wrong with your twenty-fifth left foot?' You could be likewise worried: 'How do I become peaceful?' and not realize that you are safe and doing fine— you simply need to accept and allow your mind to remain who he is—an incurable partner who'd stay with you for ever!

One of the most common questions that spiritual seekers ask is: How do I ensure that I am present in my practices? How 'do' I 'be'?

Notice the irony here—we want to 'do' our 'being'. We still haven't gotten it.

Once, during my weekly spiritual gathering, I gave a class on the glories of the Holy Names of Krishna. After the class, during the Q&A session, a person asked me on 'HOW' one could chant the Hare Krishna mantra. A lively discussion followed. I remember speaking on the principle of *sattva*, or goodness, in our lifestyle that helps us chant meditatively. The following week, another person asked me on sattva: 'HOW does one lead a sattva lifestyle?' During the discussion, I spoke about slowing down our lives. A week later, someone asked me, 'How does one slow down, given the fact that we have such a busy life?' I shared that we could possibly try some breathing techniques. And the following week, a gentleman wondered if I could share how to deal with the wandering mind when we did conscious breathing. I said chanting was the best complementary practice to breathing. And lo and behold, the following week, a curious man asked me, 'Since you spoke about the Holy Names of God last week, I am wondering 'HOW' I could chant the Holy Names?'

We were back to square one—I caught myself answering the same thing—the sattva principle that I had spoken about a few weeks ago! At that moment, I realized if I spoke on sattva now, the following week someone could ask me on 'HOW' to live in goodness. Thus, the cycle of 'HOW' to do it continues eternally!

We have let our heads trap us into being control freaks— we want to figure out the secrets of happiness; we want to do things perfectly and become happy.

Our inability to embrace imperfections and our unwillingness to accept and allow our distressed minds to coexist as we quietly march on in our spiritual path would be the cause of our downfall. Our too much worrying about not being good enough and our over analysis leads to paralysis of the mind. We get stuck and stay trapped in an overthinking cycle.

And to get out of this, we simply need to 'be'—become aware, accept and allow the mind to be with us, at least for some time daily. Make peace with who you are, accept yourself just the way you are and move on with grace.

Therefore, let us begin by agreeing to 'be' and slowing down our lives.

\* \* \*

From the next chapter onwards, we shall discuss three practices for slowing down our lives mentally. These are my daily habits of Breathe, Journal and Pray. These three methods could help you cultivate a 'being' attitude and improve your awareness and help you live in the Heart Space.

# Chapter 9

# Just Breathe: Connecting
# with God Slowly

*I see all people rushing full speed into Your mouths, as moths
dash to destruction in a blazing fire.*
—Bhagavad Gita (11.29)

The sword of death hung over my head and I saw him as an emissary of Mr Time.

The biker scrolled on his smartphone with one hand while speeding his motorbike over 80 km/hr with his other hand. The narrow asphalt road passed through a gushing stream and I faced him, feeling vulnerable. The monsoon showers abated and I was on my morning walk. In a split second, I had to decide whether to turn to my left so that he could speed away without worrying about me. But what if he saw me and instinctively turned to his right to avoid a collision? I'd meet sure death! In that case, it would be safe to jump into the watercourse below. But that would break my bones.

I had little time to choose. In an instant, I turned to my left, hoping he'd miss me. Just then, he too swerved to his right and I heard a loud siren behind me. I stood frozen as a car sped up from behind, making the breeze blow through my shirt. The bike also missed me by a millimetre. The blaring horns deafened me and in half a second, they crossed each other, mercifully sparing me from certain death.

The eerie stillness of the countryside scared me. Cuckoo birds and squirrels sang a beautiful song, while the lush mango and coconut orchards on either side of the road lent a heavenly ambience. The fragrance of night-blooming shrubs like Parijata and jasmine assured me this was a divine abode. I was, however, gripped with fear. My heart rapidly paced and my mind refused to slow down.

I had learnt the practice of slow breathing—inhale and exhale to the count of four and listen to the soft sound of incoming and outgoing breath. I forced myself to sit on a bench over the stream. After a few minutes of silent meditation with my eyes closed, I was peaceful again; the adrenaline rush had eased and my parasympathetic nervous system had awakened.

I then offered a sincere prayer to Lord Krishna, thanking Him for the close shave. Gently, I opened my eyes and saw the rivulet below carry brown sand in its speedy flow. Chappals, plastic bottles, paper, leaf plates and an occasional torn shirt passed in the stream. My attention fell on what lay below the surface. The reflection of the giant peepal tree remained unmoved, as did the thick foliage. While gushing water threw away smaller objects with disdain, some things were still.

That's when peace engulfed my heart. I knew, in a sense of knowing beyond knowing, at a space beyond the head, that, although I had a near squeak moments ago, I now seemed to live for ever. I was not this body and death didn't end everything.

*For the self, there is neither birth nor death at any time. He has not come into being, does not come into being and will not come into being. He is unborn, eternal, ever-existing and primeval. He is not slain when the body is slain.*

—Bhagavad Gita (2.20)

My close shave and the subsequent epiphany taught me a sacred lesson.

## 'Slow' Gives Spiritual Insight

If I hadn't slowed down, I'd have likely carried the fearful experience with me for the rest of the day. Or if I had busied myself with some activity and forgotten the dreadful episode, I'd have missed going deeper into my inner self. Instead, fortunately, I chose to pause and slowly connect with myself. As a result, I was now in a safe space—the area of an undying soul.

Death and suffering are realities of this world. And fear a concomitant factor. In the serene nature, we see birds picking up worms, snakes gobbling up frogs and cruel time sparing none. Yet, we constantly seek peace, often living in denial of the surety of death and suffering.

We can't afford to be pessimists, nor can we allow toxic positivity to accentuate our deep-rooted fears. The only reasonable alternative is to face and accept the reality of our fragile existence and move on with grace.

And it's here that slowness in general and conscious breathing in particular come in handy.

We are not promoting a slow movement; we only appeal to 'balance'—speed and slowness go in tandem.

## The Speed of the Mind

If you ride a Koeingsegg Jesko Absolut, you'd touch 300 km/hr. Imagine you drive a car that is five times faster on a circular road that, in turn, lays on a gigantic vehicle that speeds at 1,07,000 km/hr or 30 km/sec!

That's precisely the speed at which you and I are travelling this very moment!

The earth moves on its own axis at 1,600 km/hr and then around the sun a hundred times faster, yet each human who resides on this earthly car has a mind that wildly spins at an incalculable speed! If you let your mind imagine that you are on the sun now, you'd have travelled 150 million km in just a second! Light—with its speed of 3,00,000 km/sec—is a tiny garden snail in comparison.

And what do you think this speed does to your overall well-being? An overactive mind keeps you disconnected from your true self, just as if you ride the 'Incredicoaster' at Disneyland for just a minute, you'd feel disoriented and severed from your immediate reality. Only when you are out of it can you gather your wits.

Likewise, while navigating through the roller-coaster rides of this world, when you pause and breathe, you slow down your mind. If you drive at breakneck speed, it's not easy to keep control of the car. Life is rushing fast, but if you pause, you would not only have more control over your life, you'd also achieve more.

> *It was sunsets that taught me that beauty sometimes only lasts*
> *for couple of moments, and it was sunrises that showed me that*
> *all it takes is patience to experience it all over again.*
>                                          —A.J. Lawless

## What's the Logic of Slowing Down?

The logic is simple: When you stretch your body and perform herculean physical exercises, you're also relaxing your muscles and sufficiently resting your body. This helps you achieve the six-pack you seek and you don't burn out. Similarly, when you exert your mind throughout the day, you are brain-tired. You need to relax your mind by breathing, praying or journalling—basically just chill! The gentle switch from a relaxed to an active brain state will ensure you get the 'six-pack brain' that you want—a mind that is strong to battle shocks and navigate the bizarre twists and turns of life.

American neuroscientist Daniel J. Levitin is the author of *The Organized Mind: Thinking Straight in the Age of Information Overload*. In his talk at Google, he offered a compelling argument on how today, it's more important than ever before in human history to slow down. That's because we live in an age of information overload. As compared to 1986, today, humans take in five times more information in one day. This is equal to reading 174 newspapers. In leisure time alone, you take in 34 GB of information. All the words ever spoken by mankind amount to 5 exabytes (1 exabyte = 1 billion GB) and still, believe it or not, digital data created by humans exceeds 300 exabytes! For example, YouTube alone adds six thousand hours of videos every hour. To watch all the existing videos on YouTube, you'll need 8000 years of non-stop viewing!

We battle this overload of information with a coping mechanism called 'multi-tasking', where we try to complete two or more tasks at the same time. We assume we are smart when we switch between tabs while working on our notebook. Or we often check our WhatsApp messages and also complete our office project work or read news while having an important phone conversation with a friend. Dr Levitin explains that what actually happens is uni-tasking—we rapidly switch between tasks and our attention gets fractured. Hence, we can't concentrate for long hours and it's no wonder that ADHD is now common. Dr Levitin argues that very few jobs like air traffic control or UN translators require multi-tasking, and they also carry high risks in their occupation. That's why, in these jobs, every hour they have a fifteen-minute break because the brain can't handle so many parallel tasks. Switching between tasks releases cortisol in the brain and depletes glucose, an essential fuel for the brain. When we relax through yoga, walking or reading a book, it has a restorative effect on the brain.

What helps traffic move fast? We imagine it's the speed of the vehicles. In reality, it's the distance between the cars on a busy road that helps overall movement. Likewise, doing a lot of work in less time doesn't increase productivity as much as creating a healthy space of relaxation between two important tasks.

## How Does BJP (Breathing–Journal–Prayer) Help?

Conscious breathing helps us slowly move from the world outside of us to our inner world. As we learn to focus our attention on the soft incoming and outgoing breath, the muddle of thoughts clears up. After ten minutes of slow breathing, if you still find peace elusive, you can pick up a paper and pen and just write the proposals of the mind. Do it in the second person—as if a different person (the mind) is talking to you. For example, as I am writing this piece, I feel thirsty. My journal would appear as follows: '. . . Cancal (the name I have given my mind) is asking me to stop writing now and pick up a glass of water . . .'

You will soon notice that even before you complete the sentence, the mind has jumped to yet another demand. After completing the sentence where you acknowledge the mind's need for water, you then write the next sentence, simply noting down the next demand of Gollum (another name for my mind). Soon you'll realize that you've forgotten what the mind asked for, because by the time you completed the sentence, your mind had given over a dozen proposals. As you try to keep pace by simply noting down what the mind is saying—or what you are feeling or thinking right now—all in a second person's language, you'll have successfully separated yourself from your mind.

Journalling thus helps improve awareness—we learn to see the many noises in our head as separate from 'me'. You may wonder: If these thoughts are not mine, then who am I really? Regular practice of journalling and breathing helps you discover the answer: 'I am the one who sees that these noises are not me!'

This beautiful self, the real you, needs a voice—that's prayer. When you softly utter the Holy Names of Krishna or any transcendental sound in the sacred space of a temple, altar or silent setting, that's when you feel safe—you know you've reached Home—your Home State—or the Heart Space. That's when you see God; that's when you are with God.

The combination of Breathing–Journal–Prayer thus helps us slowly move from the madness of a speed-induced life to the serenity of graceful connection with God, Krishna.

The ancient Roman philosopher Atticus put it beautifully: 'It always pays to dwell slowly on the beautiful things—the more beautiful, the more slowly.'[8]

\* \* \*

I have journalled daily for over two decades now and would like to share, in the next chapter, the practical benefits and techniques of this sacred practice.

# Chapter 10

# Practical Benefits and Techniques of Journalling

*One who sees inaction in action and action in inaction is intelligent among men.*

—Bhagavad Gita (4.18)

My inspiration to write regular journals is the following quote by Srila Prabhupada:

*Realization means you should write, every one of you, what is your realization . . . You write your realization, what you have realized about Krishna. That is required. It is not passive. Always you should be active. Whenever you find time, you write. Never mind, two lines, four lines, but you write your realization . . . You are hearing, but you have to write also . . . This is cultivation of Krishna consciousness. Hear, write, remember and try to understand. Don't be dull, dull-headed. Very intelligent. Without being very intelligent, nobody can*

*have full Krishna consciousness. It is for the most intelligent person . . .*
   (Srila Prabhupada lecture 14 August, 1972, Los Angeles)

Three activities—conscious breathing, journal and prayer—help bring more awareness to our lives. And an alert mind is quick to smell, hear and see wisdom all around.

Journalling helps us not only discover wisdom; it also helps us store it for future reference.

If you pen down what you read and learn during your sojourn in this world, you'll be amazed by the discoveries you make in your inner world. Writing makes what you read yours.

And it helps you add to the wisdom on this planet!

When you speed on a highway, you can't figure out what's on the roadside. You may see trees and greenery, but it just passes you by. However, if the car slows down, then you could see it's a mango tree with ten branches and a crow's nest and other flower-laden trees become more visible to you. In the same manner, when you rush through life, you are disconnected from your subconscious desires and patterns; your deep-rooted aspirations and drive to bring value to the planet are unknown to yourself, let alone the world. But if you slow down your life and especially when you write a journal—about your desires and realizations—you see the minute details of your noble self. Your discovery would amaze you. You'd get more curious to explore the world inside of you.

Initially, it may seem like a scary and lonely forest, but if you continue the journalling practice, you'll see a beautiful landscape within yourself.

## Journalling Improves Self-Awareness

Right now, are you aware of the room you are sitting in? As you read this article, can you describe the place you are in, the sounds you hear and the sights you see? This is Awareness.

And Self-Awareness is a similar knowing, but of the world within ourselves.

When you are hungry, you could instinctively pull out a fruit from the refrigerator and munch to your satisfaction. But if you are aware that you are hungry, even as you seamlessly move towards the food and, if needed, you could stop your movement, you have Self-Awareness. If you are on a strict diet, your ability to recognize the pulling of the tongue and your need to stay focused on your goals is Self-Awareness in action.

Journal writing helps increase the gap between what happens to you—the provocation—and your response to it. The ability to separate oneself from his or her feelings and the knack to see our thoughts and name our feelings is Self-Awareness. It's like having an aerial view of life—seeing ourselves from a higher perspective.

And why is Self-Awareness important in modern times? Simple: You have more control over yourself.

As a young boy, I wasn't scared of my mom, even if my brothers and I did mischief. Her predictable behaviour and emotional outbursts were instinctive, and we could traverse through her anger. However, my father was a difficult man to read. A man of few words, he sent an unspoken message of being in control. If he was angry, he wouldn't raise his voice immediately. First, he would lower his voice and explain that he was angry, which was followed by silence. Then, depending on the situation, he'd express his annoyance. This was scary, primarily because it sent out a message that he was in charge of his emotions and had a high degree of awareness.

If we could improve our Self-Awareness we'd have more control over our responses to provocative situations in life. Although humans distinguish themselves from animals in their ability to make choices, many of us have become creatures of circumstance; it's as if we are helplessly dragged from one helpless situation to another. Many complain of a gnawing vacuum despite their stable lives. This has a lot to do with a persistent disconnect from our own selves.

Self-Awareness promises to once again make us creatures of choice—to improve our Heart Space by giving us more choices and control. Consequently, we are empowered to manage our inner world.

## 'I Am Not Comfortable Writing'

As kids, some of us had teachers who forced us to write essays, which we hated along with writing exams. And you may even assume you are not a writer and have no plan to author a novel or a non-fiction best-selling book. So you may profess that you have no need for writing and that you hated it as a child.

As older, free-thinking individuals, many of us still carry the same dislike for writing. I guess it brings back old memories.

But rest assured, things are different this time.

When you wrote exams, you expressed on paper what you had learnt or known. When an expert psychologist writes about the human brain, he's sharing with the world his realizations. However, when you write journals, you are writing to discover what you know.

There's a difference between writing to share and writing to discover.

Exploring our own minds and hearts is an adventurous and exciting journey. When you see journalling as a tool to enter the beautiful landscape of your heart, you'll fall in love with it!

Besides, you don't have to worry about your handwriting or perfect grammar. Your teacher may have often admonished you for mistakes in writing, but journalling is not for the world's consumption; it's your time in the Heart Space. Nobody in this world is going to grade you for your journals; you could write in different languages or use slang, and you would also not need anyone's approval. It's your private attempt to connect with yourself, therefore, no one else is judging you for it.

## What Prevents Us from Tapping the Joy of Journalling?

You may write one day and discover no earth-shattering realizations descending upon you. You get discouraged.

You try another day and the same thing happens.

When you heat water in a kettle, the electric supply is consistent. If it were to heat up the water for two seconds and then switch off the electric supply only to turn on again after thirty seconds, you'd never get warm water. It is the constant flow of current that helps the water boil. Similarly, you can't expect miracles from journalling if you cut the flow.

The secret to tapping the power of journalling is *consistency*.

Writing daily for a short time—even three to five minutes—could help you access its power. A daily commitment, albeit a small one, would help you enter your inner world.

While journalling, one day you may get scared and discover your fears and insecurities. You probably tried to avoid them all these years.

Journalling cleanses the heart and makes you come face-to-face with it. Remember, denial is the worst kind of lie, because that's the lie we tell ourselves. Since journaling uncovers our hidden fears, we might find the exercise unpalatable. But if you hang on, you'd be amazed at how beneath the superficial dirt and a scary forest is a beautiful garden of fresh flowers—your wonderful self in all its glory!

The journey to meet our own selves is the most challenging but also the most rewarding experience. And journalling promises to facilitate that.

## How to Write a Journal

I will share six common types of journalling that I practise.

The list is not sacrosanct or exhaustive; I mention them only to trigger your interest. In fact, you could get inspired to explore your own styles.

## 1. Free Writing

Some people write to share their realizations with the world. Others like me write to discover what we know.

Free writing is a great tool to discover what you know.

You pick up a pen and paper or your laptop and just write. The main thing is don't stop the pen.

Say you decide to write for ten minutes. Put an alarm and as you write, whatever the provocation, your keep moving the pen or punching the keys. If you go blank, you write, 'I am right now clueless; I don't know what I should write. But let me write something . . .'

Till you hear the alarm go off you keep writing.

This is how you 'release' and 'receive'. The baggage of the past haunts most of us. But you release the blocks by writing. We need direction for the future. We receive realizations when we write.

Free writing helps us access unknown territories within our subconscious.

## 2. Wisdom Writing

You hear an inspiring talk by Jay Shetty or Gaur Gopal and you feel rejuvenated. But soon, you forget it. And even when you were inspired, it was more of a 'feel good' phenomenon.

You know intuitively that these talks are pregnant with rich possibilities; each word spoken by the masters could catapult you to your own greatness. But it's not happening. Why is that, and how could you ensure you translate the rich wisdom available out there into your own life?

It's not happening because it's not yours! It's Gaur Gopal's realization and you simply enjoyed the talk. You first need to make it yours. When you write down what you read or hear, it becomes yours. Until then, it belonged to the speaker you heard. But when you write, it becomes yours. Remember the key here is to write not as you are hearing the talk. It's after you've seen the video. In a quiet, reflective space, you pick up a paper and pen and write your thoughts on Jay Shetty's talk. This reflection helps you access the same wisdom within you!

Often, while having lunch with the monks in our ashram, we have light-hearted discussions on life lessons from the scriptures. We are often amazed at how we discover more wisdom when we churn the existing body of knowledge.

If you reflect back on your reading, either through discussion or writing, you add to the wisdom of the sages. You may feel humble and unqualified; your own inadequacies may haunt you. Still, you are a special soul—eternal, fully cognizant and blissful—(satcitananda in Vedic parlance).

And if you have an affinity for reflection and writing, get ready for a pleasant self-discovery.

Wisdom writing is one of the most effective forms of journalling because it ensures that you learn from what you read and hear. Otherwise, the barrage of motivational videos feeds you only at the surface. They contribute little to your well-being; you could get intellectually stimulated, but you aren't satisfied.

Only when you own that wisdom is your heart nourished. And journalling promises ownership and nourishment. Aside from that, when you write, you add your own value and leave behind a wisdom legacy.

## 3. Question Answer Writing

This is a thirty-day experiment that will reveal to you your evolution and you wouldn't need others to certify that you are growing emotionally and spiritually. You will see it for yourself if you follow these three steps.

### First step: get the questions right

One day, in the quietness of your room or a garden, write down thirty questions that you'd like answers to. Keep these questions in a book or word file and revisit them later.

### Sample questions:

What does my relationship with my spouse mean to me?

Why do I get irritated by ____ and hanker to be with _____?

What drives my attractions and aversions in life?

How can I add more meaning and joy to the lives of people I love?

What are the three most important values of my life?
In this way, write down thirty to fifty questions.

## Second step: start 'free writing'

Day One—pick up Question 1 from your notebook, set a timer for ten to twenty minutes and don't put down the pen until the time is up. Keep writing and stop only when you are satisfied or when the notification rings, whichever is later.

Once you have finished writing the answer, you can read it if you like and then forget about it. Carry on with your other duties and activities.

Day Two—pick up Question 2 and follow the same procedure for writing.

Thirty days later, you'd have answered all the questions.

This ends round one.

Wait for the next morning to continue the exercise as if nothing has happened all these days.

## Third step: enter the second phase

The next day—thirty-first in the exercise—go back to Question 1 and write the answer, following the same protocol.

Now comes the discovery.

After you've finished writing or when the alarm goes off, read the answer quietly and compare it with the answer to the same question you wrote a month ago. You'd be stunned by the discovery. You will see for yourself how you have evolved.

Some answers could remain the same, while others will reveal to you that your understanding has matured. You see the situation differently. And this change is evident—in thirty days, your vision has changed. Congratulations! You are growing—the churning of your heart is a reality and you can now see it for yourself. And it is reflective writing in general and free writing in particular that has brought about this evolution.

## 4. Gratitude Journal

A one-week experiment will reveal to you the incredible power of a gratitude journal.

Write down your innermost desires without worrying about them being socially unacceptable. Just pour your heart out—what would you love to be or do if time and money were not constraints? Once you have answered this question, forget about it for a week.

For the next seven days, commit to writing a daily gratitude journal for ten minutes.

Each morning, write down expressions of gratitude to people, things, God, etc., for whatever blessings have come your way generally or in the last year, month, week or twenty-four hours.

If it feels clichéd, try 'fresh gratitude' by recalling the most moving experience in the last couple of days and expressing gratitude for the same. It could be something as silly as expressing thanks for enjoying a lovely feast of your favourite pizza or for receiving love from a friend. Don't worry if you feel grateful for seemingly ordinary things in life. After all, it's better to remember God or express gratitude for the 'ordinary' than to forget God in pursuit of the extraordinary. It's the inner wealth of gratitude and appreciation, not your lofty and abstract aspirations, that softens your heart. Get real and thank with feeling.

After a week of daily journalling, go back to the question you answered on the first day—about your innermost desires. Answer the same question now, candidly.

You'll find your desires have changed. Exactly what has changed is personal and varies for each individual. But you'll surely get more clarity, and if writing is supplemented with regular study of wisdom literature, you will rise to a reality beyond the mind.

## 5.  The Awareness Journal—the 'Now Writing'

This is the best way to break the jinx in writing. Sometimes, you may go blank and feel uninspired to write. At such times, just pen down what the mind is saying at that very moment. This is the most simple and effective way to puncture the mind's rant and also separate yourself from your mind.

For example, your reluctance to write could be because you are feeling tired. Just write that down: 'I don't want to write now because my mind is telling me that I am tired.' You'd realize that by the time you complete the sentence, the mind has given you some more instructions. Dutifully, without judging any of these proposals, just put them down. In fact, you'll be amazed at the alacrity with which the mind jumps from one subject to another; you'll not be able to keep pace with its 'most important' suggestions. But in no time, you'll realize that the mind is never satiated and, more importantly, it's not you!

## 6.  Experience Journal or 'WHY' Journal

Since the last time you wrote a journal, what has been the most touching experience you've been through?

I once saw a badly smashed vehicle and an ambulance taking the accident victims away. I soon got busy and forgot about the ghastly accident. A few days later, when I sat down to write my 'Experience Journal', I realized this accident had an impact on me. My journal took me down memory lane to the time I lost three dear friends to road accidents over a period of fifteen years. And what those friends meant to me and how their deaths taught me many lessons. And then my journal led me to examine my views on relationships and friendships. By the time I finished writing my thirty-minute journal, I realized that witnessing the recent accident had helped me recalibrate significant aspects of my life.

The key here is to first write down the event that seems important to you in terms of an experience you had. Then dive deeper into the event to see why you think the incident was important. As you dig further, you'll enter the inner world of your aspirations and value systems.

Even in your gratitude journal, if you answer the question 'why' you'll dive deeper into the ocean of gratitude. A superficial thank-you exists on the shores of this ocean. However, when you invest emotions into your gratitude, you dive deeper into the sea of abundant living to discover rare spiritual pearls that lie beneath the exciting waves of just a feel-good experience.

You could do a simple exercise now: draw two columns titled 'gratitude' and 'why'. Just express thanks for one thing that you did or that happened to you in the last twenty-four hours. Next to that phrase, answer 'why' this action or event is important for you. You'll notice that you've instantly upped the ante—your 'thank you' is no longer cursory; it's carrying the energy of emotion.

For instance, yesterday I walked on the beach for ninety minutes and felt refreshed by the early morning experience. I also spent three hours writing my next book and then had lunch with my friends from the monastery. My journal entry would be as follows:

| GRATITUDE | WHY |
|-----------|-----|
| 90-min walk at the beach | Felt refreshed and healthy. Morning walks improve my appetite and reinvigorate my mind. |
| Three hours book writing | Writing is 'me' and it's not only absorbing but also helps me share and contribute to the world. |
| Lunch with monks | Felt a deeper bonding, which makes me feel safe and at home when I am with my friends from the ashram. |

Daily experiences can teach us a lot of lessons if we only learn to pause and reflect. When we allow those events to ask and answer questions about our lives and ambitions, we learn and grow. We see a reality beyond what has happened on a particular day.

## Journalling Improves Self-Awareness but Is Self-Awareness Same as Self-Realization?

Self-awareness is the preliminary stage of self-realization.

First, there is a stage of disconnect—we are unaware of ourselves and what we really want in our lives. We are on a chariot with no control over the horses. The mind pulls us everywhere and we are a mute witness to its running riot in our lives. Journalling helps us hold the reins of the chariot of our lives; we have more clarity and control. This is the stage of self-awareness.

Self-realization is when you let go of the reins of your life again—but this time, it's not the mind, but a higher universal force that takes charge of your life. As a willing instrument in the hands of the divine, you are led to a reality and action beyond your own tiny insecurities and desires. You now choose to live for a cause higher than yourself. When you place your fragile existence in the hands of a higher intelligence, you've truly risen beyond your mind and even yourself—you've embraced the cosmic force. And this intelligence is known in different traditions by different names—Krishna, Paramatma, Brahman, Om, etc. When we surrender our lives to this person or force and live our lives in harmony with this truth, that's called self-realization.

The first step, though, is to gain more awareness. But we can't stay stuck there. Journal writing, when combined with good association and the open-hearted study of wisdom literature, leads to self-awareness and a sense of belongingness with the universe. We feel safe and one with the universe; we want to serve and feel loved—that is surrender. We let our lives be dictated by forces beyond our tiny minds.

A high degree of self-awareness with the humility to hear and learn takes us forward; otherwise, as Steven Covey says, 'Journalling without a conscience makes you a Hitler.' Adolf Hitler wrote journals regularly, but without a desire to serve and contribute to the overall well-being of others, it couldn't help much. Journalling is not a substitute for meaningful social connections; it complements our sincere effort to serve and love. That's when self-awareness helps us evolve to self-realization.

It's like making a pizza! You mix the flour with water, add a little liquid, maybe milk, and add yeast to it—you have the dough. You could then add the sauce and the toppings. Is the pizza ready? Well, almost! You still need to bake it—that's the most important step to complete the process of making pizza. Likewise, you've got all the ingredients ready—journalling, breathing, more self-awareness and a healthy, balanced lifestyle. Yet, the 'baking' remains—self-realization is when you add the right association, surrender to the Lord's will and the right attitude to serve.

## How Journaling Has Practically Benefited Me?

I have been more of an 'abstract and perceptive' kind of person. I struggled for years with logic and systems; if I had to organize a trip for our monks, I would falter. But I could discuss for hours the benefits of the trip and give a philosophical angle to it. I could speak intuitively and offer creative suggestions to make the trip exciting. I was what the traditionalists called an archetypal 'right-brained' person.

Regular journalling helped me tap the organizational side of me. I could now translate abstract concepts into doable action items. My classes often catered to the principles and theoretical aspects of our philosophy, but my daily journal helped me discover its application side. I could logically explain my stand and it was no longer simply rhetoric—I had sound reasoning to back up my presentation.

I have known a friend who was more of a 'left-brained' person—he spoke logic and had little patience to admire poetry and nature; he was a go-getter and thought linear. Journalling helped him develop his empathetic side.

Journalling can thus help complement what we lack while strengthening our innate nature. It's like being in a relationship with a perfect partner—one who makes up for what you lack and helps you get stronger in your strengths.

A friend of mine was surprised when I organized a high-profile event and a lunch programme that featured some of the most senior leaders of our community, including the presence of my spiritual teacher. The event was smooth and without glitches—every minute detail was taken care of and all those who attended were happy. When I look back, I realize that it was the practice of journalling that helped me achieve this transformation—I had surprised myself with my abilities.

The always-emotional guys—if they write regular journals—would be able to see the logical aspect of their actions. And practical men and women are able to appreciate the finer, subtler and emotional nuances of life.

During my low moments, my journal has been a great companion as well.

## How Do We Write—on Paper or An Electronic Screen?

If you love someone, you could send emojis and love texts on WhatsApp. But when you write a handwritten card or a letter, there's a special feeling—a wonderful energy of love—that you tap. In the same manner, when you write on an electronic screen, it's not the same as when you write on paper. Yet we live at the crossroads of history, and times and people have changed. So, maybe it works best for you to write on your smart phone. The essential ingredient of journal writing is connection. Are you in touch with yourself? And whatever works best for you to get in touch with yourself, do it.

The dopamine-induced electronic screens do have an inherent limitation; they can't give you the same feeling as a paper and pen. Yet, logistics may demand you write on a computer and so be it.

Besides, when you begin a journal practice, it doesn't matter—'just write' is the formula. When you want to jog because you want to lose weight, initially you may just run. As you get more proficient and regular in the practice, you may become particular about other details. And over time, if you get so hooked on jogging that you contemplate taking part in a marathon, you may even get into finer details—the viscosity of the shoes, the wrist and sweat bands, the shorts and t-shirts that you wear—all of them matter. Likewise, initially, just write. As you progress by praying and connecting to yourself, you'll discover your unique ways of journalling.

And as you progress, you may also fine-tune your practices and discover details that are best conducive to helping you connect with yourself and God. And then there are the logistics: saving paper versus storing digitally, confidentiality issues, etc.

We all have an impulsive self and a reflective self. Journalling helps us create a space between what happens to us and our responses to those triggers. As writing on paper and pen is slower, it could help some of us tap our reflective selves better.

I invite you to explore journalling as a sacred tool for an exciting journey to your inner world. You'll surprise yourself as you soon discover a better version of yourself.

* * *

*I know the benefits of all healthy practices, but still, my mind protests and refuses to cooperate. How do I make all of them a part of my daily existence?* The next chapter talks about the simple principles of making the mind a friend.

# Chapter 11

# You Could Fool Your Mind

*The living entities in this conditioned world are My eternal fragmental parts. Due to conditioned life, they are struggling very hard with the six senses, which include the mind.*
—Bhagavad Gita (15.7)

We've often heard how the mind tricks us, but have you ever wondered how you could fool your mind as well?

I learnt this technique from a dear friend, Ananda Gopal Prabhu (also known by his legal name, Ashok Nahar), who wrote the invigorating book, *5 Sutras to Form New Habits*.

I was upset at my inability to cultivate the habit of yoga, daily listening to Srila Prabhupada's lectures and book writing.

Years ago, I had practised 'stupid small steps' as advocated by Stephen Guise in his book *Mini Habits: Smaller Habits, Bigger Results*, and managed to write two books in a year. But with the power of time, lethargy crept in again. Then I read *Atomic Habits* by James Clear and learnt the method of 'Indexing–Linking–Tracking' and was inspired again. But somehow I couldn't translate my inspiration into action—I had all the good intentions but still couldn't do yoga. As the saying goes, 'there's many a slip between the cup and the lip'.

Then Anand Gopal Prabhu helped me see the mischief played by my mind.

## Principle of Simplicity

'It's not yoga that you need to make a habit of now; rather, it's the energy of yoga that you need to connect to,' explained Anand Gopal Prabhu, 'it's your subconscious mind that needs programming.'

I was interested as he explained how my desire for perfection or the need for an hour of yoga, makes it practically impossible to start the yoga practice. The mind dismisses anything that is less than perfect. 'It's simply an excuse given by the mind so that you don't do yoga,' said Anand Gopal. 'So come to terms that you are not perfect and you don't need to do one hour of yoga daily.'

He was teaching me the principle of SIMPLICITY. Keep it simple and achievable. 'Pull your yoga mat out, lie down on it, get up and just smile,' said Anand Gopal Prabhu. I couldn't believe what he said. 'This is simplicity in action and by doing this you are entering the energy of yoga. You are declaring to the universe that you want to do yoga.'

## Consistency

But there is a second equally powerful principle that can't be ignored—CONSISTENCY. 'You can't afford to miss this one-minute yoga ritual even one day. Even if the sky falls on your head, you'll do this,' he declared.

I wondered if I was very sick and how I could follow the principle of consistency. As if anticipating my dilemma, he said, 'On days you have a fever or you are hospitalized because you've broken your leg (God forbid), you can watch a YouTube video on yoga. Remember, you are entering the space of yoga.'

As the sceptic within me doubted the efficacy of the process, Anand Gopal instantly pulled out his phone and showed me the forty-plus habits he had systematically tracked and cultivated over the last two years and how he had internalized them.

## Indexing–Linking–Tracking

Impressed, I looked at him bug-eyed. I was all ears. He continued to share the most important aspect of habit cultivation. Besides the two principles of consistency and simplicity, there is a system of three tools called Indexing–Linking–Tracking, or ILT for short.

Indexing is when you write down all the habits that you wish to cultivate. I had over twenty in mind, but I mentioned to him only three of them. I sought to test the waters before surrendering to his process. After all, I still had my doubts—it all seemed too good to be true. He then asked me if I could link these new habits that I seek to cultivate with the existing ones that I have.

## Habits Unknown to Us

I wanly said I have no habits, as if I had resigned myself to being inadequate and unable to improve.

He smiled assuredly and said, 'You have at least thirty habits and I can reveal them to you if you so desire.'

Again, he had grabbed my interest. How could he be so sure I have thirty habits when I was convinced I had none?

'Do you wake up in the morning?' he asked plainly. I nodded in the affirmative, wondering what he was driving at.

'Do you sleep at night? Do you take a bath? Do you have food? Do you put on your clothes?' I smiled at his ingenuity. He was right; I had many habits. 'Now let us link the new habit that you seek to cultivate with one of your existing habits.' He said it so simply. I was amused and impressed.

'When would you like to do yoga?' he asked me, 'You need to link yoga to one of your present habits; which one would you like to choose?'

I thought for a moment and said, 'Before my lunch.'

## Simple but Not Easy?

'Daily before your lunch, you need to pull out your yoga mat and sit on it for one minute', he said conclusively.

'That's it?' I probed him.

'Yes, that's the principle of simplicity and the method of linking in action,' he said.

'But will it help me become a sincere yoga practitioner?' I asked. The sceptic in me rose again.

He saw me struggle with my mind and said, 'It's simple for sure, but not easy!'

'You are conditioned to do many things and to do them perfectly; as a result, you just can't relate to simplicity'

'Hmm', I nodded, 'but how will I know I am progressing?'

'You need to track your habits daily—and that's the third method, tracking.'

I said, 'First is indexing—where I write down the habits that I seek to cultivate. Next, I link it to an existing habit and the third step is to track it.' I was summarizing what he had said.

He said, 'Yes, and remember the two principles— simplicity and consistency; do the simple act of sitting on a yoga mat for just a minute, daily, even if you are very busy.'

## Taking a Step Back

I said, 'I am not sure I can track all of my twenty new habits daily.'

He smiled and said, 'Again, your mind has fooled you.' He explained to me patiently that although I had agreed to the simplicity principle for my habits, I was still rigid, which made my habit cultivation very difficult. 'Initially, you said you wanted to cultivate three habits and now you say you have listed twenty. You are quite ambitious and that's good. But you need to remember simplicity.'

I wondered how I was breaking the simplicity principle. He said that the fact that I want to cultivate twenty habits all at once shows how I am still struggling.

'Let's go one step back', he said, 'instead of tracking twenty habits, why don't you start tracking your tracking?'

'Excuse me?' I said, unsure if I had heard correctly.

He said, 'The only way you'll be convinced of the simplicity principle is if you start tracking only one thing for now.'

'And how do I do that?'

'Every night before you sleep, put a tick on the column of tracking. The first column is the date and the second is tracking.'

'But what exactly am I tracking?' I asked.

'You are tracking your habit to be accountable. You are convincing your mind to slow down and practise simplicity. Once you have practised this for three weeks, you'd at least get used to spending a few seconds every night, before you sleep, to track your habit of being accountable. Then, slowly, you could add three more habits.'

And things began to roll out exactly the way he predicted. After my first three weeks, I would nonchalantly pull out my tracking sheet and put a tick on the column indicating tracking.

I was now ready for tracking yoga, writing and listening to Srila Prabhupada's lectures. Regarding book writing, I simply wrote one line daily and I linked it to the existing habit of finishing my lunch. He revealed to me that these were two habits: beginning to eat my lunch and ending it. So after I finished my lunch, I chose to write one line for my book. And before lunch, I did yoga.

Regarding listening to Srila Prabhupada's lectures, the simplicity principle was to pull out the Srila Prabhupada audio device, hold it in my hand for a couple of seconds and chant the Srila Prabhupada pranama mantra. And I had the habit of checking my email at least once a day. I linked listening to Srila Prabhupada's lectures to my email checking. This was an act of connecting with the energy of listening to Srila Prabhupada's class.

Now I had both simplicity and linking in place. I had already indexed my new habits. And I had begun tracking daily for over three weeks and I simply added these three habits.

Now the last challenge was consistency—I had to do these three things daily.

## Breaking the Inertia

Is it difficult to do the simple act of putting a yoga mat on the floor and sitting on it daily? Or how long does it take to write one sentence?

One day, I was busy the whole day and had half an hour of break just around evening. I could have opened my computer and written for a few minutes. But during those days, I had a target to write a book every year and I wanted to write a minimum of 1000 words daily. As a result, when I did get time, I was discouraged by the fact that I may not be able to write as much as I desired. And I ended up not writing at all.

Then I came across the ILT method and my target now was just one sentence daily. But this had to be done every single day. A few days ago, I was down with body pain and a slight fever. I had no desire or strength to write. However, my target was just a sentence. So I reluctantly rose from the bed, trudged to my table, opened my notebook and began writing. Once I wrote a sentence, I could easily write the second one. Then, a few ideas gushed out of my head onto the computer. Soon, I was in a flow state. I ended up writing more than 1000 words and I had spent over an hour. And this was when I thought I was sick, while ironically, earlier, when I had time, I wrote nothing. This simple act of trying to write one sentence had inadvertently broken the inertia. Without intending to outsmart my mind, I had done that very thing.

That's when I realized that ILT is an amazing trick to outwit the mind.

## Mind and Gollum

Two decades ago, *The Lord of the Rings* trilogy captured the imagination of moviegoers like nothing else before it in cinematic history—the seventeen Oscars it bagged are a testimony.

Gollum undoubtedly remains one of the most fascinating characters in this series. He serves his master, Frodo, yet is wicked and attached to the ring. He is clever and can engage in riddles, but he uses them to trap victims. His perverted sense of self-love and self-hatred, his vicious anger and his scary and insatiable greed make him a perfect representative of the human mind.

Gollum is within, wreaking havoc with our fragile lives unless we learn to tame him.

And it all begins with more awareness. As Rumi said, 'If your eyes are opened, you'll see the things worth seeing.'

Now, it remains to be seen if I can use the ILT to keep my mind in check or if Gollum has the last laugh.

* * *

From the next chapter onwards, we enter the sacred world of prayer and a relationship with God.

# Chapter 12

# Surrender: The Key to a Relationship with God

*Abandon all varieties of religion and just surrender unto Me.*
*I shall deliver you from all reactions. Do not fear.*
—Bhagavad Gita (18.66)

This exercise will help you discover where you stand in your relationship with Krishna or God:

Open your mind's eye. Now, visualize a screen or board and draw a vertical line—the line of struggle.

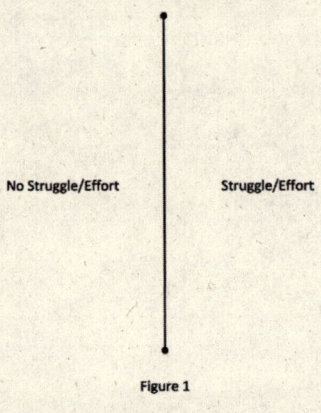

No Struggle/Effort          Struggle/Effort

Figure 1

The space on the left of the line denotes 'No struggle/effort' in spiritual life and the area on the right signifies 'Struggle/effort'.

If you believe spiritual life to be a laidback, relaxing process where we simply follow what the mind says, then you are likely living on the left of the line. I have known people who said, 'I'll practise spiritual life someday in the future' or 'I'll come to your temple when God invites me.'

In our tradition, Srila Prabhupada gave us a simple spiritual process of chanting, dancing and feasting on sanctified food called *prasada*. Some members imagine spiritual life to be free of any kind of struggle. They may misquote Srila Prabhupada, 'Just enjoy Krishna Prasad and attain perfection in spiritual life.'

## The Line of Struggle

If you are spontaneously attracted to an easy spiritual life and to Srila Prabhupada's pastime, where he glorifies the ease of spiritual practice, then you are well established on the left of the vertical line. Once, when devotees expressed difficulty in perfecting their spiritual lives, Srila Prabhupada humorously declared, 'Just hold on to my dhoti and I'll take you to the spiritual realm—I have a key through the back door.' On another occasion, he said, 'While impersonalists struggle in their spiritual practices, we go back to Krishna's (God's) kingdom, simply by eating a gulab jamun (an Indian sweet)'.

Those on the left of the line are easy-going and not inclined to take up the anxiety of struggle or more responsibility in spiritual life.

Those living on the right of the line quote Srila Prabhupada, saying that spiritual life is extremely difficult and one has to practise rigorous discipline. They are attracted by the austerities and fasting. They chant more, perform herculean tasks and take on more challenges—they believe struggle is the name of the game. They quote Srila Prabhupada, who once said, 'If I told you how many gallons of tears you have to shed to get Krishna, most of you'd run away.' The seemingly difficult practices excite you if you live on the right side of the line. Here, you try to control the mind and you are determined to go back to God's abode in this lifetime, maybe even tomorrow. You have a sense of urgency.

Decide where you are more naturally situated: to the left or the right of the vertical line.

Remember, we are not discussing where you should be situated or what the ideal state should be right now. We are understanding what 'is' and not what 'should be'. We are taking an honest stock of our relationship with God and not learning how to improve it.

Once you have chosen your position, erase and forget this illustration from your mind's screen. We'll come back to it later.

## The Line of Surrender

Now, in your mind's eye, imagine an empty space and draw a horizontal line—the line of 'Remembering God' or the line of 'surrender'.

**Remembering God**

_____

No Rememberance of God

**Figure 2**

Let us see which side of this line you are on.

If you spend days or weeks forgetting God, with no prayer and only tasks to do, then you are living below the line. 'I've been so busy with such important responsibilities that I had no time to pray or remember God.' If this is your common complaint, you are firmly settled below the line of 'Remembering God.' You may be busy with fifty things to do in a day and you may tick all the boxes, but there is no heartfelt offering of your emotions to God; you are disconnected from Krishna.

Those above this horizontal line call out to the Lord often. They spontaneously think of Krishna. Srila Prabhupada said that he'd fly kites with his sister as a child and pray to Krishna, 'Let my kite fly higher.' Although remembering Krishna for flying a kite is seemingly an ordinary act, the act of connecting to God places you above the line.

Decide where you live most of the time—above or below the horizontal line.

## The Four Quadrants of a Relationship with God

Now, let us merge both Figures 1 and 2.

You have four quadrants in this new image in your mind.

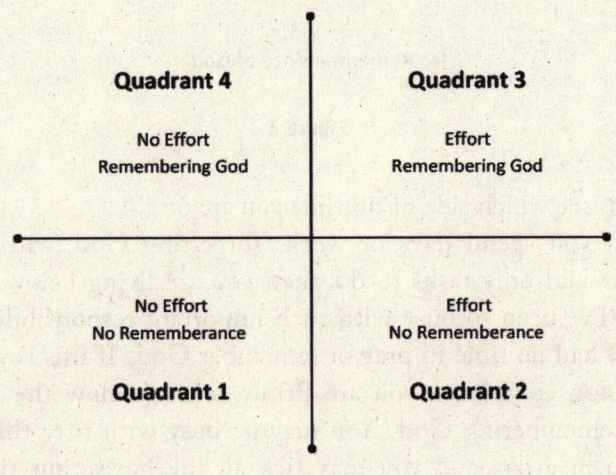

**Quadrant 4**

No Effort
Remembering God

**Quadrant 3**

Effort
Remembering God

No Effort
No Rememberance

Effort
No Rememberance

**Quadrant 1**

**Quadrant 2**

Figure 3

On the bottom left, we have Quadrant 1—the space of no effort and no remembrance of God (Krishna).

On the bottom right is Quadrant 2—effort/struggle and no remembrance of Krishna.

On the top right, we have Quadrant 3—the area of struggle/effort and remembering Krishna.

On the top left is the space of Quadrant 4—no struggle but total dependence on Krishna.

When you drive a car, you know when and how to change gears. Similarly, as you drive your spiritual life, you can know which quadrant you are situated in and accordingly move higher up.

At any given point in time, simply ask a question: 'Which quadrant am I in right now?'

## Lifestyle in Four Quadrants

### Quadrant 1

### Relationship with God—Non-Existent

Those living in Quadrant 1 neither remember Krishna nor invest the concerted effort to progress in spiritual life. Of the three modes of nature, it is *tamas*, or mode of ignorance, that binds them tightly. This is when illusion gets us and we end up doing things that betray our own values. This is a zone of sense gratification, where our mind drives the chariot of our lives.

Bhakta Das drives his car on a highway and it breaks down. If he lives in Quadrant 1, he'd simply lament and curse the road or shout expletives.

Since he neither remembers God nor makes an effort to serve God, his relationship with Krishna is non-existent.

### Quadrant 2

### Relationship with God—Passive

A Quadrant 2 lifestyle is characterized by sincere effort and hard work. But the essence of Bhakti Yoga is to always remember Krishna and a practitioner fails on this front. Although it takes only a few moments to sincerely call out to God in love, our busyness sucks the nectar of remembering God from our lives and we live with faith in our own abilities more than God's help. Amongst the three modes, it is *rajas*, or passion, that binds a practitioner here. While in Quadrant

1, it was his mind that held the reins of the chariot of his life, here in Quadrant 2, one's intelligence is active. He plans, organizes, studies and takes charge of his life. But again, God is conspicuous by His absence and instead of sense gratification, now it's a zone of struggle. You are holding the reins of the chariot of your life; you are in charge and you struggle.

Bhakta Das, if he lived in Quadrant 2, would call a mechanic and somehow manage to get help. He'd focus on solving the sudden crisis asap. He has faith in his own abilities and doesn't consider depending on Krishna.

He is making a journey closer to Krishna by making some effort. Since he is externally a devotee, he does render some services to Krishna, albeit unaware of Krishna's love and omnipotence. Even if he intellectually knows Krishna to be the Supreme Personality of Godhead, he still doesn't believe in or trust Krishna's protection. Therefore, he doesn't remember God favourably and his relationship remains passive.

## Quadrant 3

### Relationship with God—Active

Quadrant 3 is when you add the element of sattva, or goodness, because now you have begun to take shelter in God. You remember Krishna while you continue the struggle. Your intelligence is active, yet you are also adding the principle of depending on Krishna in your life. You've begun to realize that it's difficult to do things on your own—a lot of things aren't in your control.

This is the ideal stage of our spiritual practice, where we make the effort and also remember God with love.

Krishna asks Arjuna to remember Him and also fight the war (Bhagavad Gita 8.7). He was asking Arjuna to position himself in Quadrant 3.

As you manage your busy schedules and fulfil your various responsibilities, you also remember Krishna. You offer your heart to the Lord and continue to put in more determined efforts. You are active and find happiness in your spiritual practices because you've added the critical element of remembrance of Krishna.

If Bhakta Das lived in Quadrant 3, he'd remember Krishna by offering a prayer and simultaneously calling for help. He'd do both and thus maintain spiritual consciousness even amidst a sudden reversal of his plans.

He has begun a relationship with God now. He connects to Krishna with his mind and heart. This favourable remembrance of God makes our hearts grow with positive emotions and our relationship is now active.

Spiritual practices for most of us mean changing gears and moving from Quadrant 1 or 2 to Quadrant 3. While the first two quadrants are the spaces of sense gratification and struggle, respectively, the space of Quadrant 3 is struggle plus shelter—we have touched Krishna with our mind and intelligence.

In Quadrant 3, you still hold on to the reins of your life's chariot, but you are also calling out to the Lord for help.

A friend shared an interesting realization:

'In my new job, I saw my boss had a large framed photograph of Shaun, his Doberman, on his desk. Intrigued, I asked him about his pet and he got emotional. He explained that his dog had died and that they were really close. Now, his memory nourishes him and the photograph on his table reminds him of Shaun. Being a new member of ISKCON at the time, I had begun associating with devotees and was trying to figure out how I could tangibly experience God in my day-to-day life. Shaun inspired me. I brought my favourite deities' photographs and kept them on my table. In the midst of the day-long office work, I would take short breaks, for a couple of minutes, and connect to the Lord on the framed photograph on my desk and get back to work again.'

This is Quadrant 3 living—we struggle and we also remember the Lord.

A life centred on Quadrant 3 drags us seamlessly to Quadrant 4. Sooner or later, situations and challenges fall upon every spiritual practitioner. Bhakti Yoga practices lead us to totally depend on God. Surrender is the natural culmination of a life centred on sincere devotional service.

## Quadrant 4

## Relationship with God—Sweet Surrender

Quadrant 4 is an impeccable journey for those who are firmly established in Quadrant 3. God personally orchestrates the life of a sincere devotee who seeks to remember the Lord favourably. He will guide us and take charge of our lives if we simply increase and improve the quality of our remembrance of the Lord—that is, live more often in Quadrant 3.

A sincere spiritual practitioner realizes at some point in time that he is helpless and Krishna's mercy alone can save him. He'd let go of his struggle and depend fully on God. The horses in his chariot are going wild and he gives up control to rein them in. He surrenders to Krishna and allows the Lord to take over his chariot.

**Relationship with God**

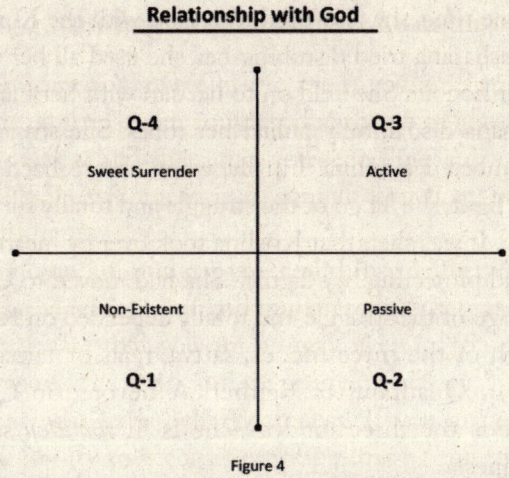

Figure 4

Externally, a person in Quadrant 4 appears similar to one in Quadrant 1—both let go of the reins of their life's chariot. The critical difference, however, is that a Quadrant 1 passenger has allowed his mind to take charge, whereas a Quadrant 4 rider depends on God/Krishna (known in different traditions as 'the force' or 'universe' or cosmic intelligence). He surrenders to this person or energy and places his life under the command of a force bigger than his own mind and intelligence.

If we live in Quadrant 3, Krishna will guide us to Quadrant 4.

If we predominantly live in Quadrant 1 or 2, we'd find Bhakti Yoga practices hackneyed. Our spiritual life would be dull and unexciting. Or worse, we may derive pleasure in fault-finding and gossip; we'd deprive ourselves of a deep, meaningful connection with Krishna.

The best example of a Quadrant 4 scenario is Draupadi. When she learnt she was lost in the gambling match and was summoned to the royal assembly, she instantly prayed to Krishna.

At the same time, she also tried to reason with the Kuru elders. When Dushasana tried disrobing her, she used all her might to protect her honour. She held on to her sari with her hands, even as Dushasana disdainfully pulled her robes. She struggled and also remembered Krishna. Finally, when she realized she was losing the fight, she let go of the struggle and totally surrendered to Krishna. It was then that Krishna took over by incarnating as the sari and protecting her dignity. She had moved to Quadrant 4—she let go of the struggle and totally depended on Krishna.

Which of the three modes, sattva, rajas or tamas, drives a person in Quadrant 4? Neither! A devotee in Quadrant 4 transcends the three modes—she is in *shuddha* sattva, or pure goodness.

## A Healthy Relationship with God

Your relationship with God is healthy when you live in Quadrant 3. This is where you begin to remember Krishna. This is where you connect with the Lord. When and where you move to Quadrant 4 is your personal journey, orchestrated beautifully by the Lord.

When your car breaks down, you could be in Quadrant 3—you seek help and also pray to Krishna. But imagine you are in a plane and the pilot announces that both engines have failed, but he is trying his best to navigate the plane to safety. What would you do, then? There is nothing you could do physically. You could now choose to move to Quadrant 4—helplessly call out to the Lord.

All of us, at different times, face situations that overwhelm us. Our efforts and intelligence fail, and we need the shelter of a power beyond our own. When we 'surrender' to this force, known in our tradition as Krishna, we are moving to Quadrant 4—the zone of surrender.

Going back to the chariot analogy, in Quadrant 4, like in Quadrant 1, a person gives up the reins of the chariot of his life. But this time around, it's not his mind that drives his life; he has placed his fragile life in the hands of his eternal lover and well-wisher, Krishna. God takes charge and the devotee watches his dear Lord pull the strings of his life. A devotee in Quadrant 4 is a happy and willing puppet in the hands of his puppeteer, Krishna. There is no more struggle in his relationship with God—it's now in a space of sweet surrender.

In this material world, surrender has a negative connotation. People imagine the act of surrender to mean losing independence, being subjected to slavery or other unpalatable and disagreeable terms and conditions. In our spiritual practices, however, surrender is a sweet expression of offering our heart and life to our beloved Lord. Devotees experience God's loving embrace and emotional fulfilment when they surrender to God's will.

In this essay, we learnt to see where we are and we could accept our existence in either Quadrant 1 or 2.

In the next essay, we will study how, with the culture of prayers, we could rise to live in Quadrant 3 or Quadrant 4, and how we could increase and improve our surrender to God and thereby experience a more fulfilling life.

\* \* \*

The journey from Quadrant 2 to Quadrant 3 happens when we add the element of remembrance of God. And a favourable remembering of God is called prayer. To make prayer effective and, in turn, help us move to Quadrant 3 and eventually to Quadrant 4, we need to internalize six practices. The next chapter helps us dive into the subject of the six steps in a prayer.

# Chapter 13

# Six Steps of Prayer

*Those who fix their minds on My personal form and are always engaged in worshipping Me with great and transcendental faith are considered by Me to be most perfect.*
—Bhagavad Gita (12.2)

To maintain a meaningful connection with a loved one, it is crucial to experience love in the relationship. Similarly, for those who practice Bhakti Yoga, it is essential to perceive the presence of God in their lives. This experience is necessary to continue one's spiritual practices.

How can we feel God's presence in our daily lives?

## Six Steps to Connecting with God

Here are six steps that can help us connect with God on an emotional level.

These are three principles and three specific, actionable methods (a total of six steps) that can help us touch Krishna or God with our emotions; we'd then feel His presence to be a veritable reality.

## The Three Principles

The first three principles are Trust, Scriptures and Listening.

These form the foundation on which the three actionable steps rest.

1. Trust: invest time and energy in spiritual practices and take on more responsibility.
2. Scriptures: connect with an intelligence higher than our own mind–ego nexus.
3. Listen: practise present-moment awareness and mindfulness.

## Step 1: TRUST: A Life Beyond Knowledge and Belief

Many people believe that to experience God's love, we need to know more about God. While knowledge is important, it is not the defining criterion for experiencing God. There are scholars who know about God but do not believe in what they read to be true.

### From Knowledge to Belief

During an academic convention, a PhD professor shared with one of our devotees the minute details about God found in our scriptures. When the devotee expressed surprise and asked how he knew the specifics of Lord Krishna, the professor revealed that he had studied Krishna for over two decades. However, the devotee felt a little uncomfortable when the scholar pulled out a cigarette with a glass of wine already in hand. Understanding the devotee's predicament, the professor chuckled and said, 'Oh, I see that you are remembering the four vices of Kali. I may be earning residence in a couple of hells for my present action.' He had no qualms about what he was doing; he even rattled off the names of a few planets where he would be thrown disdainfully by the agents of death for breaking the universal laws. He even quoted verses from the Bhagavad Gita.

After the meeting, the devotee left with the realization that real knowledge is not simply knowing the information contained in the books. One needs to believe in and practice what one reads to experience God.

Many religious organizations exhort their members to 'believe' in God. They gather thousands for mass baptisms and fervently appeal to their loyalists to believe in their messiah or their interpretation of God. Often, it's pep talk that psyches people up, and the most common thing heard from evangelists and fanatics is the chant, 'I believe in God.'

When I ask myself, 'Do I truly believe in God?' the answer that resounds in my heart is a big 'Yes.' However, I still feel inadequate. Am I willing to take bold steps to come closer to God? Am I prepared to invest time in Krishna consciousness and improve the quality of my spiritual practices?

Do I fundamentally trust God?

## From Belief to Trust

When you jump out of a plane, your parachute should open. But what if it fails?

Is it possible to feel safe as you take a leap into the unknown? As a believer in God and one who finds the verses of the Bhagavad Gita sacred, trusting in God and these texts requires action. This involves taking steps, such as performing more acts of service or spending time chanting His Holy Names, which demonstrate an implicit faith that God cares for us—that's 'jumping with the parachute'. Taking these steps can bring about a spiritual experience that is more than just an intellectual conviction.

Trust is a personalized belief displayed through the actions we take to serve God and humanity. With a quiet, inner assurance that God will safeguard us, we can jump into the unknown and feel secure. God is our eternal well-wisher.

Just as in a romantic relationship, feeling loved and safe requires trust. If our partner knows our likes and interests and believes in our abilities, we feel confident. But when our partner trusts our intentions and love, we feel loved and secure. Similarly, we may believe in God's ability to protect and care for His devotees, but do we trust Him to protect and care for us personally? Can we honestly say, 'God loves me'? If the answer is yes, God is convinced that we love Him and that is significant. However, if the answer is no, we must take steps to place more trust in Him.

I noticed the owner, a big, heavy-set man, standing behind the cash counter of a plastic chair shop while I chatted with the young customer care attendant. As the conversation progressed, I realized that the young man was quite knowledgeable about the chairs, so I asked him if he truly believed the chairs were strong enough and would last for many years. After he assured me, I asked him, 'But do you trust them?' He looked at me curiously and I lightened the conversation with a tongue-in-cheek comment: 'If your proprietor stood and jumped up and down on this chair, I'd know for sure that he trusts this chair.'

If you want to trust God, you need to take baby steps to make tangible deposits in your relationship with Him. This is beyond just an abstract sense of love.

To attract Krishna's love, you need actionable steps and that's when scriptures come in handy.

### Step 2: SCRIPTURES—An Intelligence Beyond Our 'Mind–Ego' Nexus

Studying wisdom books from various traditions can be compared to analysing military textbooks.

A friend of mine who graduated from the Indian Military Academy studied various subjects, including science and warfare, military history and the tactics and techniques of war. I was fascinated by his wealth of knowledge about famous and lesser-known battles in human history, so I asked him how his studies would help him during a real-time war. He explained that the books he read provided valuable insights into the strategies, tactics and decision-making processes of past military leaders. The course aimed to develop well-rounded officers who could understand and address the complex challenges of modern warfare, ensuring their instincts were sharp enough to make the right decisions during a particular war.

I likened his experience to that of a spiritual warrior who studies scripture. Wisdom books from various traditions provide valuable insights into the experiences of saints and struggling aspirants. As we sincerely read them, we learn to navigate life's challenges with greater understanding and purpose.

A rookie soldier has a narrow experience of war, but when he studies military textbooks, his perspective broadens. Similarly, a novice in spiritual practices may take his mind–intelligence–ego too seriously and feel constricted in his growth. However, by reading inspiring stories and examples from wisdom books, he learns about men and women who faced similar challenges to our own. This learning helps him navigate through life's myriad challenges, develop a moral compass and seek comfort and solace. And during a particular provocation or stimulus, he would act in alignment with his vision and purpose.

Regular reading of the scriptures means we trust an intelligence higher than our own to guide us in our spiritual journey. Studying scriptures also demonstrates our humility and willingness to access this higher dimension, where we consider God, or Krishna, to reside.

We will explore the subject of scriptures in greater detail in the next chapter.

## Step 3: LISTEN—Mindfulness in Prayer

In a healthy relationship, expressing your heartfelt emotions without the fear of judgement is vital. However, it is a two-way process, which also requires actively listening with an open heart. Similarly, in our relationship with God, we must also learn to 'listen' by paying attention to the sounds and silence within ourselves. When we chant sacred mantras, we should listen to the sound they create. When we pray at the altar or in a sacred space, we pause and 'be' present, hoping to hear what God wants to communicate to us.

Prayer is not just about communicating our desires to God; it is also about allowing God to communicate with us, sharing what He wants for us. However, if we live in our heads and do not take the time to listen, we will miss out on the messages that God has for us. Therefore, 'pausing and listening' is an essential practice in spiritual life.

In the Hare Krishna movement, we incorporate the element of 'listen' by focusing on the sound of the *Hare Krishna* mantra during our prescribed rounds of chanting on our beads. As we chant softly and finger the beads, our minds may wander, but we gently bring our attention back to the syllables of the Hare Krishna mantra to maintain focus.

Additionally, during other activities such as attending classes in the temple, interacting with other devotees, greeting the deities or participating in sankirtana—congregational chanting of the Holy Names—we seek to 'listen' and remain present in the moment.

Following the first three steps, as mentioned above, means creating a culture that makes connecting to God easy.

As you try to get these principles in place, the three techniques discussed below will help you have a profound experience of God.

## The Three Techniques

The three techniques are: **Commitment, Execution** and **Return and report**.

These are three practical methods that can help us experience God, provided we get the foundation of the three principles that we discussed above, in place.

4.  Commitment: a promise of a specific practice
5.  Execution: follow-up on the promise
6.  Return and report: be accountable to God

## Step 4: COMMITMENT—A Promise of a Specific Practice

If you connect with scriptures and are mindful as you participate in spiritual services within a community, you may experience moments of epiphany. It could be during a prayer, chanting session or listening to a class, and you might feel inspired. Take note of that moment and that experience, and make a commitment to God.

Invest emotions as you promise Him about a specific action that you would undertake to please Him.

For example, one morning, during the prayer session, I was inspired to make a commitment to the Lord that I'd appreciate at least five other members of our monastery. Later, when we greeted the deities, I consciously made this commitment, just as I would promise a friend. Knowing that I would return to the temple altar in two days, I promised to fulfil my commitment of sincerely appreciating five devotees in the next forty-eight hours.

This step helps us view God as a person, a sentient being who listens and waits for us. He is pleased to reciprocate our devotion. To experience His reciprocation, I need to communicate with Him as a person and promise Him, as I would to a person in this world, something specific that I will do for His pleasure.

## Step 5: EXECUTION—Follow Up on the Promise

Inspiration strikes like a flash, with great intensity, but it can just as quickly disappear. That's why Step 4 is crucial—it helps us capture the inspiration by making a promise, allowing the spiritual motivation to linger a little longer in our consciousness. However, the mind can be fickle and easily jump to something unholy with equal ferocity, causing us to forget the promise we made to Krishna in no time.

This is where Step 5 comes into play—it plays a critical role in our efforts to experience God. In my own experience, I tried to appreciate some of my friends and when I genuinely did it, I knew I was building my self-worth and improving my relationship with God. I was honouring my word, and I felt happy and grateful for the opportunity to fulfil my commitment to Krishna.

However, soon enough, the pressure of many 'things to do' and various other commitments took its toll. I forgot my obligation to Krishna and became busy with many other activities. Occasionally, I did remember, but the intensity of my work led to instant forgetfulness of my purpose and relationship with Krishna.

When I finally reached the temple as scheduled, forty-eight hours later, I just didn't remember my promise. I met a few friends in the temple and carried on with my other activities. It wasn't until later, while talking to a friend, that I suddenly remembered I had not fulfilled my promise. I felt a sense of failure—I had let myself and Krishna down. My mind quickly dismissed the commitment exercise for Krishna as futile.

For many weeks after that, I never made any promises to Krishna. It seemed like the process didn't work.

But then I realized that I had missed the most important sixth step of the process.

## Step 6: RETURN AND REPORT—Be Accountable to God

Years ago, a student promised to chant four rounds of the *Hare Krishna* mantra on his beads daily, but then, soon after that, he stopped attending my classes. Three months later, he called to tell me he had been chanting for the past week. I was happy to hear from him and asked how he had been doing. He explained that he had avoided me because he felt like a failure for not fulfilling his promise. I reassured him that it was okay and that he wasn't obligated to chant a certain number of rounds daily.

This reminded me of my own experience with Krishna when I failed to honour my promise to appreciate five devotees. We often avoid people who make us feel bad about ourselves and when we fail to keep a promise, we fear judgement. However, God is not like the fallible and judgemental people of this world. He doesn't judge us if we fail to honour our promises to Him. He is happy when we return to Him.

That's why the sixth step, 'return and report', is the most important. When we come back to Krishna, we feel His love. Especially when we think we have failed and yet we return and explain what happened and how we still love Krishna and want to honour our promise to Him, we experience non-judgemental acceptance. This is why God has been glorified across all traditions for millennia—He's the only one who loves us despite all our failures.

Returning to Krishna helps us find shelter. When we confess our failures or report our successes and genuinely seek to serve and reconnect with Him, He loves us back unconditionally. This happy experience of connecting with Krishna reinvigorates a spiritual seeker to make fresh promises with renewed determination to please Krishna.

Over time, being accountable to Krishna and reporting to Him personally helps a practitioner find deep emotional fulfilment in Krishna consciousness.

## Srila Prabhupada's Example

Srila Prabhupada set a personal example of how to develop a close relationship with Krishna.

In the early 1970s, he faced numerous challenges while building a temple for Krishna in Bombay (now Mumbai). One of the major obstacles was a man named Mr N, who tried to cheat the devotees and even sent goons to evict them from the land. He also spread malicious rumours about the Hare Krishna movement through pamphlets. However, Srila Prabhupada remained resolute in his determination to keep the land and build the temple. Despite some of his disciples losing heart and even cancelling the deed, he insisted on retaining the land and eventually succeeded in obtaining legal possession.

Some of his disciples were puzzled by his unyielding attachment to the land, but they did not understand the depth of his relationship with Krishna. Srila Prabhupada had made a personal promise to Sri Sri Radha Rasbihari, the deities at the Bombay temple, that he would build a temple for them. He fought tenaciously against the crooks, who sought to take away Krishna's land as a way of keeping his promise.

Five thousand years ago, when Lord Krishna appeared in Vrindavan, His parents, Nanda and Yashoda, were constantly worried about His safety from the demons who often attacked the village. Similarly, Srila Prabhupada took it upon himself to serve and 'protect' Krishna by building a temple for Him. He lived on the basis of a personal relationship with Krishna.

In 1970, Srila Prabhupada made a similar promise to the Sri Sri Rukmini Dwarakadish deities in Los Angeles. Even though they were being worshipped in a small storefront at the time, Srila Prabhupada envisioned a grand temple for them. He kept his word and built a magnificent and ornate temple that now attracts thousands of visitors each year.

## Coming Back to Krishna

Srila Prabhupada taught us that making a vow to Krishna is a serious matter, and that one should only do so if they are fully committed to keeping it. He emphasized two principles: making a promise to Krishna under the guidance of a spiritual master and avoiding vows that are too difficult to fulfil. It's better to make a small promise and keep it than to make a big vow and fail to do so.

Srila Prabhupada was also compassionate and accommodating when devotees failed. He acknowledged that the path of Krishna consciousness is not always easy and that it's natural to sometimes struggle or fall down. However, he stressed the importance of rectifying our mistakes and returning to Krishna through practical measures like chanting more or associating with sincere devotees.

To cultivate devotion and commitment to Krishna, we must make sincere promises to the Lord and honour them. Even if we fail, it's essential not to fall away but to rise and come back to Krishna. By honouring our commitments, we can experience profound love for Krishna.

However, unlike Srila Prabhupada, we may sometimes find it challenging to keep our promises to Krishna. During such times, it's crucial to remember that Krishna loves us and what matters most is that we return to Him and maintain a healthy emotional connection with Him.

\* \* \*

In the next chapter, we shall explore three principles that nourish a life of prayer: Smallness, Scriptures and Servitude.

# Chapter 14

# Three Sacred Principles of Prayer

*Always chanting My glories, endeavouring with great determination, bowing down before Me, these great souls perpetually worship Me with devotion.*
—Bhagavad Gita (9.14)

In this chapter, we shall explore three principles that nourish the life of a monk's prayer, as emphasized in our monastic tradition of Bhakti Yoga: Smallness (sankirtana), Scriptures (*Srimad-Bhagavatam*) and Steadiness.

## 1. Be Small, Be Positive

*Though it may seem paradoxical, recognizing our insignificance can lessen our worries.*

Self-help gurus often teach us to be positive to alleviate stress and anxiety by propounding mantras such as 'Believe in yourself' or 'You can do it'. Why not try a different approach for a change? Like saying, 'I am small and loved by God' or 'I belong to Krishna and am safe in the universe.'

One day, I witnessed the efficacy of this approach. I was sitting under an almond tree and gazing at the open sky. As horns blared from cars stuck in Mumbai traffic, the birds above flew gracefully back to their homes. The orange orb of the sun gave way to the stars and the moon in a clear night sky. Were these things telling me something? I saw an occasional plane twinkle with red and yellow lights, smoothly gliding upwards till it seemed to be swallowed by the heavens, the plane and its passengers tiny in the expansive world outside it. I, too, felt small and humbled.

The next morning, I was on a plane to Perth, flying 7000 miles away from home. As the plane finally began its descent, I looked at the city below. Its skyscrapers appeared no bigger than dots on paper. I wondered about the people who lived there—people who had their own share of worries and needs. But at 30,000 feet, looking at the stretch of land below, I felt their tragedies evaporate; their issues were non-existent.

Later that night, as I lay in bed, I again saw, this time through the window, the huge sky with its moon and stars. Suddenly, I felt connected. Were they not the very same stars and moon that I'd contemplated twenty-four hours earlier in that crowded and noisy Mumbai street? They had travelled with me and I had so many friends up there. I felt a sense of belonging to the universe. I was indeed insignificant, so tiny in the face of this huge cosmos, yet, in a sense, I felt loved; I felt connected. I suddenly realized I knew who I was: I was inconsequential, yet I had a special place here and beyond.

## Who Are We in the Universe?

Since that day, I have tried occasionally to connect to the principle of being small yet loved by God, of feeling safe in my relationship with the universe and of being at home in my Krishna conscious practices. These attempts at connection have had a much more pronounced effect on addressing my worries than the plethora of motivational self-talks available online.

Images of planet Earth from space show a tiny dot amidst countless heavenly bodies. And it's so amazing that in that miniscule point exist my country, my state, my district, the street where I live and the small apartment I reside in. How much more insignificant are the worries packed into my little head in comparison to the gigantic cosmos?

What happens when we choose to become small? What's the science of it all?

## Srila Prabhupada's Magic Formula

To be part of a big plan is a refreshingly different paradigm than to be the centre of the universe. Srila Prabhupada taught us this principle through the process of sankirtana, the congregation chanting of the holy names of Krishna.

The Vedic scriptures recommend that for the modern day and age, the practice of sankirtana is most effective for spiritual emancipation. To tap its power, we place ourselves as an instrument in the Lord's plan, one insignificant member of the Lord's transcendental army. As Hare Krishna devotees chant and pray collectively in *kirtanas* (glorification of the Lord), they feel a sense of belonging; they know that although each of them is a miniscule part of Krishna's plan, they are embraced by Krishna and nourished in their relationship with Him.

Srila Prabhupada appealed to us to connect to Krishna, who is a reality beyond our body, mind and senses. Often, we are so preoccupied with our problems that we fail to see the beautiful reality beyond our small existence. Sun—the gigantic ball of fire is many billions of times bigger than a tiny piece of metal. Still, when close to our eyes, a small coin can block our vision of the colossal sun. We are often so engrossed in our daily worries that our sight of the big picture, which is life, is blocked. Yet our larger vision of life is a far more significant reality than a colleague's harsh comment or the shrieking expletives of a haughty passerby.

## Lesson from *Śrīmad-Bhāgavatam*

For an ordinary person, hardly any calamity can equal the prospect of meeting death. But Emperor Pariksit, who was cursed to die by snakebite within seven days, saw the larger plan of the Lord and also saw himself as an instrument in the Lord's scheme of things. Therefore, when many saintly people appeared on the scene to honour him, he was unfazed. Knowing that an extraordinary event would happen, sages from different planets arrived, for the king had renounced all his material wealth to take complete shelter in Krishna. Yet the king offered prostrate obeisance to the sages and declared that they were respecting him because his grandparents were glorious devotees of Krishna. He claimed he had no qualifications. He claimed that he was insignificant, like a place where people wash their feet before entering a house.

This mood of the king attracted Sukadeva Gosvami's arrival on the scene, as a result of which the immortal *Śrīmad-Bhāgavatam* was spoken. Sukadeva Gosvami is considered the greatest example of kirtana, and Pariksit Maharaja exemplifies the mood of its best participant. He took shelter with the sages and asked for their blessings to serve devotees, get attached to the Lord and be friendly with other living entities. He sought the shelter of the Lord and was happy to receive the poisoned bite of the snake–bird. Death didn't matter; the glorification of the Lord was all-important to him.

## Application in Our Daily Lives

How does the 'be small, be positive' principle translate to my daily reality? How can I heal my anxieties based on the practice of glorifying the Lord?

As I briefly mentioned in the first chapter of this book, the December 2004 Tsunami revealed the power of sankirtana. The tsunami had left the men and women shaken and feeling helpless, and it all happened in a few minutes. Indradyumna Swami's programme of sankirtana was an instant hit. People smiled and danced. After a few days, as the team prepared to leave the first village for the next, the villagers surrounded the devotees and insisted they stay for some more days. Finally, there was a tearful farewell. The sankirtana had captured the hearts of the suffering people; it gave them hope and happiness.

Our daily lives are beset with worries. Worry is like a bird that flies above our roof. We can't really prevent that, but we can stop the bird from building a nest there. The strength to thwart the mind's attempt to build an anxiety nest comes when we spend quality time daily in a space beyond the mind and senses. That space is sankirtana—the space of God.

## 2. *Śrīmad-Bhāgavatam* (Scriptures) and the Search for Fulfilment

*Simply by one's giving aural reception to Śrīmad-Bhāgavatam,*
*the feeling for loving service to Krishna, the Supreme Personality of*

*Godhead, sprouts up at once to extinguish the fire of lamentation, illusion and fearfulness.*

—*Śrimad-Bhāgavatam* (1.7.7)

What is common to Robin Williams, Virginia Woolf, Kurt Cobain, Ernest Hemingway and Nafisa Joseph? You might not recognize all these people, but all of them had their claim to fame before their tragic and premature deaths. The cameras flashed, people eulogized them and suddenly, it was all over.

While die-hard optimists might shrug off these examples as exceptions to the general rule of money and fame leading to happiness, careful observation reveals otherwise. Unhappiness is a common feature of modern life.

While the rich and famous continue to put up the façade and assure us all's well, we find a classic parallel to the modern tragedy of discontentment in Vedic history.

The most accomplished writer and poet of all time sat on the bank of the river Saraswati wondering where he'd gone wrong. Srila Vyasadeva had composed not only the voluminous Vedas, Mahabharata and Upanishads, numbering over a million verses, but he had also delineated steps to achieve mastery in manipulating matter. The eight mystic perfections, such as becoming smaller than the smallest, getting whatever one wants at any time and developing special skills to increase beauty and wealth, were all known to him. He would be renowned as the most proficient writer from then on, with no mortal coming close to his achievements.

Yet, an emptiness engulfed his heart and he pondered over the root cause of his dissatisfaction. Logically it didn't make sense because, through his unparalleled works, he had immense access to all that one considers synonymous with happiness in this world.

As Vyasadeva sat despondent, Srila Narada Muni, his spiritual master, arrived on the scene. In an interesting conversation between them that's elaborately described in the first canto of *Śrīmad-Bhāgavatam*, Narada teaches his disciple that real fulfilment comes only when we lovingly connect with and glorify Krishna, the Supreme Personality of Godhead. As long as we are absorbed in the nonspiritual aspects of our lives, especially in the pleasures this world offers us, we'll feel a gnawing vacuum in our hearts.

## Finding Nectar in Matter

Why is someone attracted to Bollywood, Hollywood, cricket, football or politics? Or why does a mango or a dish of ice cream excite us? Because these phenomena contain a *rasa*, or 'juice', that pulls us towards them. We are not usually pulled by the colour or shape of the mango; it's the essence carried by the fruit that tempts us. Whether relationships, news, events, hobbies or anything else, practically everything in this world carries a rasa that makes it appealing.

Unfortunately, all rasa of this world follows the law of diminishing returns: the more we increase our consumption of something, the more we experience a decline in the satisfaction we derive from it. When you eat a sweet, initially you may crave more. But as you take a second and third helping, you'll feel less desire for the sweet and eventually stop consuming it. In a romantic relationship, couples go gaga over each other at first but soon realize it's not easy to tolerate each other's idiosyncrasies. Mushy expressions change to daily rifts and squabbles; soon the 'juice' is out of the relationship.

## Problems Worsened by the Mind

While everything in this world has a unique taste, it's limited. The inherent attractiveness fades after a while. Besides, our mind has an inexhaustible appetite to feast on negative experiences. From a mixture of mostly happy events, it expertly picks up one unpleasant incident and chews it with the gusto of a teenage boy chewing bubblegum. Having drained all the juice out of the gum, the boy can only blow bubbles to extend his happy experience. Similarly, the devil within us relishes a taste of grumbling over a failure or perceived injustice by the boss, which can abruptly throw us into an angry mood that we also try to enjoy. Although the juice is out of the event, the mind, desperate for more, swells it and blows it far beyond proportion.

What would happen if the teenager were to inflate his bubble beyond a certain limit? It would explode on his face. He'd then have to clumsily pick up each strand of the stuck gum. If we don't check the mind's bubble, which is often cut off from reality, it will likewise get stuck on our consciousness, requiring us to remove its sticky mess from our psyche, a task more difficult than removing bubblegum from our face.

Even the mind follows the law of gravity; we slip to lower consciousness, as if naturally. Fortunately, spiritual activities and connection to God offer an anti-gravitational thrust and offer us a healthy alternative to being victimized by the mind's games.

## Krishna: The Embodiment of All Rasas

A fish taken out of water will suffocate even if you give it the latest iPod, designer jeans or pizza. Water is the natural environment for the fish; likewise, Krishna is the space where the soul finds shelter and safety. We belong to the spiritual realm and are part of God. The material world is foreign to us and all endeavours aimed at satisfying our bodies and minds will only prove frustrating.

Narada Muni diagnosed the cause of Vyasadeva's despondency in these (paraphrased) words: 'You have written many books, but in none of these have you sufficiently and exclusively glorified Krishna as the Supreme Personality of Godhead. All kinds of literature and activities that do not intend to glorify the most attractive pastimes of Krishna and please His transcendental senses can never satisfy us. Besides, I consider such pursuits to be a waste of precious time.' (Srimad Bhagavatam, 1.5.10-11)

Narada reasoned that we should refrain from squandering our rare and valuable human form of life by occupying our time and energy with bodily and mental activities. Our real identity transcends these bodily designations and if we connect ourselves to Krishna, the supreme transcendence, we can experience a natural state of happiness.

As parts of the Supreme Lord, we constitutionally seek rasa. It is our desire to relish this taste that attracts us to enter any relationship or pursue any activity.

Krishna, the Supreme Personality of Godhead, is defined as *akhila–rasamrita–murti*, the source and embodiment of all rasa. When we connect with Krishna, our taste increases with the passage of time.

This is in stark contrast to the rasa contained in matter, which wanes with time. For example, devotees in the Hare Krishna movement chant the same *Hare Krishna* mantra every day. Some devotees have been chanting *Hare Krishna* for the past five decades. Imagine singing the same song or poem daily. Wouldn't it get boring after some time? When you read the news, you want the latest. If I hand you last year's newspaper, you won't be interested. However, we daily read about the same pastimes that Krishna performed 5000 years ago. And we don't feel a need to tweak the storyline—say, by having Krishna descend from a helicopter to vanquish His enemy Kaliya. There is no need to change anything about Krishna. His rasa gets better with each day and that's because He's the personification of all rasa.

We learn from Lord Chaitanya Mahaprabhu's biographers that He heard the history of the great devotee Dhruva Maharaja many times and each hearing of the same narration from *Śrīmad-Bhāgavatam* increased His spiritual joy. In contrast, when we watch the same movie or read a sports or film magazine more than a couple of times, we are saturated.

## *Śrīmad-Bhāgavatam*: Identical to Krishna

Srila Narada Muni, therefore, advised Vyasadeva to broadcast the messages of Krishna without hesitation. Thus, Srila Vyasadeva composed *Śrīmad-Bhāgavatam* at his most mature stage of realization. This work contains the immortal nectar (*rasamrita*) of Krishna and His dealings with various devotees. In each of the twelve cantos, Vyasadeva described the pastimes of Krishna and His avatars in detail. *Śrīmad-Bhāgavatam* is considered identical to Krishna. It is His literary incarnation. It gives us the same benefits we'd get from His direct, personal association.

Narada Muni predicted that the sincere glorification of Krishna would cause a spiritual revolution in the impious civilization of the world. He assured Vyasadeva that descriptions of Lord Krishna, even if filled with literary discrepancies, would transform people's hearts and fill their lives with unlimited happiness.

## Srila Prabhupada's Gift of Krishna

Srila Prabhupada reveals his own humble state of consciousness in one of his purports to the conversation between Narada Muni and Srila Vyasadeva:

> We know that our honest attempt to present this great literature conveying transcendental messages for reviving the God-consciousness of people in general and respiritualizing the world atmosphere is fraught with many difficulties. Our presenting this matter in adequate language, especially a foreign language, will certainly fail and there will be so many literary discrepancies despite our honest attempt to present it in the proper way. But we are sure that with all our faults in this connection the seriousness of the subject matter will be taken into consideration and the leaders of society will still accept this due to its being an honest attempt to glorify the Almighty God.
>
> (commentary on *Srimad Bhagavatam*, 1.5.11)

The evidence of the potency in the honest presentation of *Śrīmad-Bhāgavatam* is seen in Srila Prabhupada's own preaching. In the USA, where Srila Prabhupada established his movement in 1966, he faced an audience that included mostly young people absorbed in sensuous pursuits and many of them were addicted to truly harmful habits. Moreover, he spoke English with a Bengali accent and he was almost fifty years older than the boys and girls he was teaching. Yet he could transform their hearts in an almost magical way. Like a benevolent pied piper, he attracted thousands of young people with the love of Krishna he carried in his heart.

During his initial days in New York, Srila Prabhupada discoursed on Lord Chaitanya Mahaprabhu's teachings to Sanatana Gosvami. Some of the students attending his class wrote notes, penning Sanatana's name anywhere from 'Sonton' to 'Suntan'. Despite the language challenges, Srila Prabhupada's heart resonated with love for Krishna as he filled the world with Krishna's message and love. The fortunate souls who were willing to tune in to these vibrations caught the transcendental infection of love for Krishna that Srila Prabhupada carried and distributed profusely.

In less than a dozen years, Srila Prabhupada spread the message of Krishna consciousness across six continents. As an ambassador of the spiritual world, he came to invite us to the beautiful world of Krishna, where the rasa of Krishna gives one succour and the strength to face the repeated onslaughts of material energy. The pages of *Śrīmad-Bhāgavatam* thus call us to experience Krishna rasa and fill the hole in our hearts with the complete whole.

Armed with the weapons of sankirtana and *Śrīmad-Bhāgavatam*, we need another one—steadiness—to complete the trio of tools that enhance our life of prayer.

## 3. Steadiness in Spiritual Practice—a Lifelong Commitment

*Commitment is what transforms a promise into a reality.*
                                                    —Abraham Lincoln

'YOU HEARD my wife shouting at me?' He gaped in disbelief.

I had unintentionally overheard their conversation when I forgot to disconnect my phone while it was in speaker mode. I placed it on the table, and as I resumed writing, he too put down his phone on while driving the crowded roads of Mumbai. The busy traffic kept him glued to the steering wheel, and he didn't realize that he hadn't disconnected. A few moments of silence passed when suddenly I heard his wife's voice boom on the phone.

'You'll now go and spend an hour with Prabhuji while I sit in the car waiting for you!' She sounded angry.

I had been speaking to her husband, my close friend and schoolmate for many years, to request that he come to my room for some time to discuss some devotional service we were doing together. They were driving home, and he had consented to meeting me. I had no idea she would be upset. She went on with her tirade for another five minutes—the mess their house was in, the maid's tantrums, the house tasks he hadn't completed. She gave him a piece of her mind while he intermittently nodded and sounded a soft 'Hmm'.

I heard every word with keen interest. I knew I shouldn't eavesdrop, but the temptation was hard to resist. After some time, I hung up.

Later, as promised, he came to my room and he was restless, all the while keen to go back to his waiting wife. Since we have been good friends for many years, I thought of playing a prank. I urged him to stay on for a longer time and he sheepishly made excuses. Finally, I mischievously smiled and confessed that I had overheard her rebuking him. I even apologized. He was incredulous.

I exclaimed, 'She really was upset with you.' To which he simply sighed, saying, 'Oh Prabhu, that wasn't even a trailer.'

A few days later, we met again, this time in a more relaxed setting. He recalled the incident and we laughed over it. He candidly confessed that he shares a loving relationship with his wife.

'She is very caring', he said gratefully, 'but sometimes she also purifies me with this aspect of her personality. I guess I make too many mistakes and irritate her too often.'

He was more philosophical and confessed, 'I guess marriage has opened my eyes to the reality that love is not simply about sweet exchanges; she isn't only whispering sweet nothings in my ear. She also corrects me.'

## The Honeymoon Phase of Spiritual Life

We then discussed how the same principle applies in our relationship with Krishna and especially in our chanting of the holy names.

Devotees in the Hare Krishna movement chant a fixed number of rounds of the holy names daily on their beads. Initially, many of us were only 'interested' in the process of Krishna consciousness and we chanted when we felt like it or when it was convenient. But over time, we made a commitment to chant regardless of how we felt or whether or not it was convenient.

As new practitioners, we were often excited and imagined that spiritual life in general and chanting in particular would always be ecstatic. Some of us thought we'd enjoy Krishna consciousness forever and that our lives would have no more problems.

But, as we discovered, soon the honeymoon phase is over. Krishna, like a loving spouse, begins to show us the mirror. The first benefit that chanting *Hare Krishna* offers a sincere practitioner is the cleansing of consciousness. When you clean your room, it's hard work. It's going to be intense when we chant and purify our hearts as well.

Just as you clean the dirt from your room, similarly, when we invite Lord Krishna into our hearts by chanting His holy names, He also mercifully cleans our hearts. And He kindly allows us to see the dirt-like, unhealthy aspirations there. In the beginning, we are motivated to chant and the process is exciting, but later, it's commitment that keeps us going. A wake-up call for those who had a romantic idea of Krishna consciousness, this realization comes as a rude wake-up call. It's like my friend feeling cared for by his wife, but that doesn't mean she spares him her frank feedback. Devotees feel loved by Krishna, yet they feel the pain of their own inadequacies. They realize that their relationship with Krishna isn't always sweet like kheer, but rather it's more like a sweet-and-sour vegetable dish—different yet still irresistible!

And this realization keeps the devotee humble. Thus, humility is not a contrived principle or a skill that one develops. Rather, it's a gift that Krishna gives when He sees we are sincerely willing to keep the relationship going, cheerfully and gratefully. When we come to terms with our limitations, accept ourselves the way we are and yet offer our tiny existence to Krishna, we come closer to Him.

When I understand my frailties and yet trust that Krishna will help me in my spiritual journey, I attract His grace. I feel loved by the Lord when I seek to come closer to Him by purifying my heart of my lower desires.

Krishna helps a devotee feel loved, but the process He has given us also humbles us. This humility is Krishna's gift when He sees we value our relationship with Him.

## From Excitement to Fulfilment

A relationship with your loved one will have its ups and downs; there will surely be moments of exhilaration, yet you may feel frustrated. Likewise, there will be occasions when you chant and dance in ecstasy, yet the element of hopelessness is also there. Krishna consciousness has its share of austerity, as one performs devotional activities consistently for years. Devotees chant for decades with faith and humility, and they do experience a sense of belonging with the Lord. It's a fulfilling relationship, but it may not always be a stimulating one.

In modern culture where happiness is equated with the titillation of the senses, deep fulfilment in our bonding with Krishna may not appear attractive at first. Therefore, Krishna entices devotees with thrilling kirtanas, succulent prasada, grand festivals, exciting challenges and uplifting yatras (pilgrimages). But to practice the process for years calls upon spiritual practitioners to commit to their relationship with Krishna. The little choices we make daily to chant, pray and remember Krishna, regardless of what's happening in our lives, will eventually lead to the final result of the love of Krishna that we are striving for.

A married couple soon realizes that there is more to love than the fun and frolic of the courtship days. Love demands tolerance, forgiveness, understanding, patience and many other qualities. In the same manner, initially, Krishna consciousness is all about fun—because it's about how I enjoy and do what I like. But as we go deeper into our relationship with God, it's about pleasing God according to His terms.

## Definition of a Spiritual Practice

Sadhana, or spiritual practice, has three elements. First, it is a long-term practice. It isn't a two-year or even a ten-year project. Devotees practise the process for many decades, diligently and enthusiastically. Second, there is no interruption in the practice. Whether it's hot or cold, whether they're happy or sad, sincere spiritual practitioners (*sadhakas*) keep up their daily practices without interruption. And third, there is an investment of emotions—sadhakas offer their intention to please Krishna.

After an initial stimulating period of discovering the process, a newcomer is ready to take the plunge and deepen the relationship with Krishna. Just like the archetypal 'boy meets girl and both are happy to marry', ideally, a new devotee in the Hare Krishna movement, soon wants to become a serious, committed devotee.

And we express our sincerity by making a commitment. We are willing to give our time and energy for the remaining part of our lives in order to develop a deeper relationship with Krishna.

A new sadhaka aspires to take spiritual initiation and just as a Vedic wedding includes a fire sacrifice and an exchange of vows, a spiritual *diksa* (initiation) includes a practitioner's vowing to follow regulative principles. In ISKCON, the sadhaka also vows to chant a minimum of sixteen rounds of the Hare Krishna mantra on beads daily. In a marriage ceremony, a boy and girl who claim to love each other commit to each other. Similarly, devotees receiving diksa commit to their guru and express their serious intent to make their relationship with Krishna a lifelong one. In this world, too, without commitment, we cannot experience the depth of any activity or relationship. Therefore, devotees commit to their relationship with their guru and Krishna and aspire to make their lives a preparation to enter an eternal life with Krishna in His kingdom, the longed-for home of the soul.

## Shabari's Dedication

The Ramayana describes the committed services of Shabari. She chanted Lord Ramchandra name constantly and as her guru, the sage Matanga, was leaving this world, he assured her that one day the Lord would come to receive her service. Thus, Shabari waited for many decades for the Lord to arrive. She chanted and prayed with enthusiasm and eagerness to receive the Lord, who eventually granted her His audience.

In our conditioned stage, we may chant for a few decades and wonder how long it will take for us to experience the pure love of God promised in the scriptures. Commitment means remaining steadfast in our promise long after the mood in which we made it has left us.

Shabari teaches us the attitude of commitment. She was blissful as she patiently waited for the Lord to reciprocate.

The Ramayana also describes in detail the beautiful trees and fragrant flowers that bloomed in Matanga Rishi's ashram. There was a secret to these flowers, which remained ever-fresh. The residents of the ashram would daily go to the forest to fetch firewood and other ingredients for their daily worship. They worked hard and served their guru sincerely. When the sages returned after an intense and satisfying day of service, drops of perspiration from their bodies fell on the ground. As soon as a drop of sweat touched Mother Earth, it instantly transformed into a beautiful flower that never wilted away. It remained fresh forever. The disciples' loving offering of service to their guru caused this phenomenon.

Similarly, Srila Prabhupada's dedicated years of service to his beloved guru's mission brought about dramatic changes in people's lives. His labour of love and his perspiration that came out in the form of his books and discourses transformed into fragrant offerings of love. Each year, thousands of people find inspiration to dedicate their lives to Krishna and they remain as fresh as ever.

## Exemplary Commitment to Service

Haridasa Ṭhakura chanted 3,00,000 names of the Lord daily. When he got older and was unwell, Lord Chaitanya Mahaprabhu asked him to reduce his chanting. Yet, Haridasa Thakura was hesitant to give up his vow. Lord Chaitanya reciprocated Haridasa's commitment by allowing him to leave this world in His presence the next day.

Another exemplary associate of Lord Chaitanya, Sanatana Gosvami, circumambulated Govardhan Hill in Vrindavan daily as part of his service to the Lord. During his old age, he continued his service, although it was physically challenging. Lord Krishna then appeared and gave him a special stone from the hill and asked him to offer his worship to this stone instead of the hill. These stalwart devotees have shown us the way to committed spiritual practice. When spiritual practices are performed in this spirit of perseverance, the practitioner's journey culminates in going back home to the Godhead.

And until then, while feeling loved by Krishna in our spiritual practices, we also keep discovering our flaws and inadequacies. This keeps devotees humble. Simultaneously, Krishna fills the devotee's heart with a sense of belonging to Him.

As for my friend, I suggested he spend more time with his family. I could manage our shared services on my own. His wife happily agreed.

\* \* \*

Spiritual practices are never easy. The mind rebels and the material energy is unflagging. We need shelter.

*Bhakti Yoga is all about rendering service and beseeching the Lord for grace.*

The next two essays explore how a spiritual practitioner learns from a soldier, a beggar and from a dog.

# Chapter 15

# Are You a Soldier
or a Beggar?

*Those who are on this path are resolute in purpose and their
aim is one. O beloved child of the Kurus, the intelligence of those
who are irresolute is many-branched.*

—Bhagavad Gita (2.41)

A young warrior brandishing an AK-47, with adrenaline
pumping, marches confidently to battle. His seniors and
comrades encourage him to fight the enemy known as Maya,
or the illusory forces in this material world. He is confident
and roars at the enemy, shoots a few bullets in the air and
believes his friends, who assure him that he will emerge
victorious. He is young and determined to win the war against
Maya and go back to the kingdom of the spiritual world. He
preaches fearlessly and chants determinedly; his weapon is
his bead bag; his shelter is the association of devotees. His
shooting bullets is akin to preaching and serving fearlessly.

A few years pass in a happy Krishna consciousness life.

Then one day, suddenly, he sees a bullet of serious doubt
whizz past him. It was a close shave, and he feels shaken.

Then another bomb of faith-shaking scandal or controversy explodes—he barely manages to dive to safety. He then takes guard and adjusts his gun (bead bag), even as various temptations and distractions threaten to pull him away from spiritual life. He looks behind him for those who egged him on to march into the war. He sees no one! A realization dawns: 'I have to fight this battle alone.' He has friends and spiritual support in the Krishna conscious community, but still, it's his battle; he has to fight all his scuffles alone!

All these years, while he was flaunting his bead bag and preaching vigorously, Maya hadn't taken him seriously.

But now she is determined to finish him.

## Winning the War

As he fights this unrelenting enemy, he feels weak, disappointed in his own inadequacies and also discouraged. Nevertheless, he puts up a brave front; after all, he's a gritty spiritual warrior. He truly believes he can win this war. However, secretly, he hopes and prays that Maya has pity on him and spares him the daily battles. He is getting battle-weary.

One day, he reads about how Srila Haridas Thakur was tempted by Maya personified, with all her enticing grandeur. He had known this pastime all these years, but now, for the first time, he realizes that Haridas Thakur chanted 300,000 names every day, and he chanted them attentively. And yet, he wasn't spared from Maya's attacks. 'And here I am, struggling to stay awake in my Japa', wonders our combatant, 'and I expect Maya to be lenient?'

## The Wake-Up Call

This is a wake-up call. He realizes this is not an ordinary skirmish, but a lifelong war. A few battle victories do not excite him anymore because there's always the next time when Maya will attack. The more successful we are in our devotional service, the more tests and challenges await us.

He fights harder, struggles to perform more austerities, takes on more responsibilities and busies himself with day-long services in the hope that he'll have no time for Maya. But Maya secretly smiles at our fighter's foolhardy attempts, as she has unlimited tricks up her sleeve. Her arsenal of temptations and distractions to draw a spiritual practitioner away from Krishna is endless. Her ubiquitous presence in this material world and her quiver of unending arrows make her the most overwhelming archer, and our tiny soldier is no match for her.

## The Out-of-the-Box Solution

This is the time to think outside the box. Our weak fighter needs to give up the soldier's robes and adorn a beggar's demeanour.

You may have looked at a beggar with an 'up-down' approach, with compassion and benevolence. But have you ever looked at a beggar with a 'down-up' approach, where you see from his point of view and relate to him at his level? Have you desperately sought someone's generosity? Since many of us have not beseeched favours frantically in this world, we aren't effective 'beggars'. We have pride in our abilities and our false ego would rebel at the prospect of seeking clemency.

A sincere Hare Krishna practitioner takes on the mood of a 'beggar' and begs Krishna to allow him to serve the Lord. He is eager to please Krishna and feels personally weak and helpless. While fighting Maya bravely, he knows he is simply a beggar. This dual role of a soldier and a beggar is a paradox that an intelligent devotee learns to accept as part of his devotional lifestyle.

The 'soldier' devotee now reads the same Haridas Thakur pastime and realizes that Haridas Thakur begged the Lord for mercy—he considered himself a fallen and an insignificant insect, compared to all other devotees who are stalwarts, worthy of his worship. Now the fighter who relished the jokes and anecdotes in a *Śrīmad-Bhāgavatam* class finds the mood of a 'beggar' more appealing. He listens carefully to the prayers of exalted devotees mentioned in the pages of *Śrīmad-Bhāgavatam* and Chaitanya Charitamrita.

## From the Head to the Heart

This is the time we move from the 'head' to the 'heart' space in our spiritual practices. For long, we devised strategies to counter Maya's nefarious designs. We had faith in our abilities and determination. But over time, we realize that time is more powerful than our most well-intentioned efforts. It's our sincere aspirations that alone can attract Krishna's mercy. Krishna, if pleased by our desire to reconnect with Him, would empower us to face Maya's attacks with grace and fortitude. As our hearts bathe in the sweet yearning for Krishna's love, we learn to see Maya for who she is—an agent of Krishna, entrusted with the thankless task of testing us.

## A Warrior Turned Beggar from History

History has witnessed the famous test of a devotee.

In the mid-sixteenth century, when Lord Chaitanya Mahaprabhu performed His most enchanting pastimes in the coastal holy town of Jagannath Puri in eastern India, the emperor of the land was attracted by the Lord. But the Lord tested him.

Maharaj Prataprudra was an able king with widespread influence and power. He repeatedly requested his guru, the wise Sarvabhauma Bhattacharya, for an audience with the Lord. Bhattacharya was a renowned scholar and teacher, whose fame equalled that of Brahaspati—the spiritual master of the gods in heaven. He humbly petitioned Lord Chaitanya to bestow His mercy upon the sincere king. The Lord dismissed the king as a materialist, unworthy of His time and attention. Bhattacharya assured the Lord that Prataprudra was not an ordinary king but a sincere devotee who loved to serve devotees. Yet, Chaitanya Mahaprabhu was unmoved; in fact, He threatened to leave the place if anyone ever made such requests of him.

Devotees tried many indirect and direct ways to get the Lord to shower His mercy upon the king. While the Lord remained indifferent, the king, too, was determined to win the Lord's favour. One day, he shocked the devotees with his letter, in which he declared:

*If Gaurahari, Lord Chaitanya Mahaprabhu will not show mercy to me, I shall give up my kingdom, become a mendicant and beg from door to door.*
                    —Chaitanya Charitamrita (*Madhya Lila* 12.10)

King Prataprudra loved the Lord and personally served all the devotees of Chaitanya Mahaprabhu with great happiness. He pleased the Lord when he swept the street in front of Lord Jagannath's procession, and his taking this menial position reconfirmed to Lord Chaitanya that the king was a sincere servant of Krishna and devotees.

The king also happily relieved his subordinate, Ramananda Raya, who served as the governor of the Madras Province but was eager to join Chaitanya Mahaprabhu's service. Ramananda explained how the Lord wanted him to resign from his government duties and spend time with Him, chanting and hearing Krishna's pastimes. An ordinary man would have felt insecure or envious to note that while his junior is earning the Lord's favour, he is being ignored; in fact the Lord declared the king to be a materialist and said it would be abominable for Him to meet the king. Yet, the king spontaneously celebrated Ramananda Raya's good fortune and encouraged him to serve Lord Chaitanya Mahaprabhu. The king also continued his salary and humbly wished he too would soon receive mercy from the Lord.

The king wasn't spared even a public humiliation by the Lord when, during the chanting and dancing in front of Jagannath's cart, Lord Chaitanya Mahaprabhu fell in the arms of the king. This was the first time both were seeing each other face-to-face. Time stood still, as this was the culmination of many months of intense separation that the king had felt from the Lord. However, much to the king's shock, Sri Chaitanya Mahaprabhu declared that it was pitiful that he had touched a person interested in mundane affairs.

Later, when the king gave up his kingly robes and put on the simple clothes of a Vaishnava mendicant, massaged the Lord's lotus feet and sang beautiful prayers glorifying Krishna, the Lord was moved.

But the final test remained.

## The Final Test

The Lord, in great happiness, asked him who he was. At this time, the king could have introduced himself as the emperor, who had tried many times before to meet the Lord. The king, fixed in his spiritual identity, humbly presented himself as a servant.

> *The king replied, 'My Lord, I am the most obedient servant of Your servants. It is my ambition that You will accept me as the servant of Your servants.*
> —Chaitanya Charitamrita (*Madhya Lila* 14.18)

In a dramatic story with many twists and turns, as recounted in Chaitanya Charitamrita's *Madhya Lila*, Chapters 1–25, the king finally wins the Lord's favour.[9]

What is noteworthy in this episode is the king's moving away from his position as a royal warrior and administrator to that of a humble servant.

Often, we identify ourselves with our external designations of birth, caste, gender, ability, qualifications, beauty and social media presence. But to win the Lord's favour, one needs to move away from these limiting titles and focus on our inherent nature as servants of the Lord. Just as water is liquid in its constitutional position or a chilly is hot or sugar is sweet, likewise the living entity—you and me, the soul—is a servant of the Lord.

When we play the 'beggar' role, we seek to realign to this original nature of ours—we want to be a servant of Krishna. And when we happily serve the devotees of Krishna, we please Krishna and convince Him of our intentions of restoring our relationship with the Lord.

This is what Emperor Prataprudra did. And a devotee who humbly serves all and cultivates the mood of a beggar becomes dear to Krishna.

## Resolving the Paradox

A sincere devotee of Krishna is both a soldier and a beggar. He is a beggar because the 'control' of a soldier now makes way for 'surrender' of a beggar. In his inner life, he moves from the 'achieving' mode to 'receiving'; in the world of prayers, he begs for mercy. A soldier gets medals, but a beggar is 'insignificant' and receives either compassion or neglect. The reality is that we need kindness, not honour. Besides, no one is threatened by a beggar.

As soldiers, we fight the mind's lower nature, and as beggars, we make peace with our mind and beg for mercy from Krishna. Sometimes, as soldiers, we could become tough and our spiritual emotions get buried. But as beggars, we seek love and compassion from Krishna.

Srila Prabhupada writes in the preface of his book titled, 'Krishna, the Supreme Personality of Godhead', "The art of focusing one's attention on the Supreme and giving one's love to Him is called Krishna consciousness." Therefore, a devotee aspires to give his or her heart to Krishna.

And a devotee fights the war against Maya, but now as a servant of Krishna and for Krishna's pleasure.

* * *

*Once we struggle and surrender both as soldiers and as beggars, we can now have a blissful relationship with God like a dog has with his or her master . . .* This is the final relationship dynamics we explore in the last chapter.

# Chapter 16

# Spiritual Lessons from a Dog

*But those who always worship Me with exclusive devotion, meditating on My transcendental form—to them I carry what they lack and I preserve what they have.*
                                              —Bhagavad Gita (9.22)

*An evolving relationship with street dogs inspires thoughts about progress in devotional service to Lord Krishna . . .*

Over a dozen dogs snarled, ready to gnaw into my flesh. They barked ferociously, and I had only my bead bag to protect me. I felt helpless. Suddenly, from nowhere, an autorickshaw pulled up and I jumped in. It was a close shave.

It was early morning and I was walking to the village temple when the dogs surrounded me. I was overwhelmed. I guess they felt threatened by me, an intruder. Or perhaps my dhoti and kurta (rare clothing even in Indian villages these days), the tilak on my forehead and my loud chanting aroused their wrath.

The following day, I again wished to go to the temple before sunrise. This time I carried a stick, but when I saw the dogs at a distance, I retreated. I felt unsure of its efficacy to ward off the menacing animals.

A neighbour suggested I carry some biscuits. They were abundantly available at the roadside shops. I bought a few packets, and the following morning, braved the journey to the temple again. I was nervous, but the technique worked. The dogs wagged their tails in approval. I followed the ritual daily, and soon the dogs became my good friends. One day I tried another route, where previously a lone dog would bark ominously at me. But I was surprised that even before I took out my biscuits, he ran to me, happily wagging his tail. Maybe his friends told him about me, and I was a good man now!

Over the next few days, I witnessed another incident that touched my heart deeply. One of the dogs started following me to my house. I threw him a few crumbs, but he wouldn't nibble them. He kept wagging his tail, rubbing his face on my leg and jumping up, even as I briskly walked home. I wondered what he wanted. I threw some more morsels. He gave a cursory look at the scraps and insisted on walking with me. I had never liked dogs and could never touch them or allow them to come close to me. But this was a different experience. I suddenly felt like this dog wanted me to pat him. I did it instantly, and he licked me. He lifted his face up; he wanted me to love him and caress him. Grateful, he left after some time. I returned home humbled and moved by this animal's love.

## Three Levels of Our Relationship with God

Later that night, I reflected on the way my relationship evolved with the street dogs.

First, I saw fear and anger in their eyes; then, I saw that they were greedy for food; and then, I saw that this particular dog wanted only love. The third level—love—at which this dog approached me had the most profound effect on me. I wondered at how this dog didn't want any food but only love.

I realized that this is the way my relationship with Krishna needs to evolve. During my initial days in Krishna consciousness, I was sceptical and challenged every facet of the philosophy. It was as though I was barking at devotees and allowing my atheistic propensities to growl at Krishna as well, because I felt threatened by the fear of losing my enjoyment and independence. In time, as devotees showed kindness and gave me prasada, I saw that they were friends and wanted to give me love. I wagged my tail and was happy to be chanting and dancing. I often expressed gratitude to devotees and Krishna.

But my interaction with the loving dog reminds me that I need to take my spiritual life to the next level. Just as I was moved to see him reject everything else and only seek my love, Krishna will be moved when I approach Him without any material desires. When I can tell Krishna that I don't want any of the material crumbs He can throw at me but only His pat and loving embrace, then He will take my bhakti offerings seriously.

## Choosing Krishna over Material Gifts

History is replete with examples of devotees who chose Krishna's love over the material gifts He offered. Arjuna and Duryodhana approached Krishna for help before the Mahabharata war. When Arjuna arrived, he saw that Krishna was resting, and that Duryodhana was waiting nearby for Krishna to wake up. Arjuna quietly sat at Krishna's feet, while Duryodhana sat impatiently near Krishna's head. When Krishna woke, His eyes first fell upon Arjuna, and He spontaneously asked how He could serve him. Duryodhana interrupted, saying that he had arrived first and thus deserved the first offer of help. Krishna insisted that He had seen Arjuna first; moreover, Arjuna was younger and deserved to be asked first.

Krishna then offered two options: His entire army would fight for Arjuna if he wished or he could instead choose Krishna, who would not pick up any weapon. After Arjuna made his choice, the other offer would go to Duryodhana. Without batting an eye, Arjuna said that he preferred Krishna; he didn't want Krishna's army but His friendship, even if that meant Krishna would not fight. Duryodhana couldn't believe his eyes. He got exactly what he wanted—Krishna's resources. He had no liking for the person, Krishna. Arjuna, however, had no desire for Krishna's material gifts; he preferred His loving association.

Duryodhana represents a typical materialist who 'sits on God's head'; he wants to play God's role and seeks to exploit nature's resources for his own selfish agenda. Arjuna represents a typical devotee who is happy to situate himself at the Lord's lotus feet, waiting patiently for the Lord to bestow mercy, seeking only His love.

Duryodhana internally rejoiced at his great luck but externally feigned disappointment and said he'd accept his fate. He gleefully returned home, internally thanking Arjuna for his 'foolishness'. But as events unfolded later, Arjuna's choice proved auspicious, and the Pandavas won the war largely due to Krishna's timely intervention at practically every step. Although Krishna lived up to His promise and didn't fight, he orchestrated events to help Arjuna and the Pandavas.

## Srila Prabhupada's Instructions

Dhruva, a five-year-old boy, was determined to get a kingdom greater than Lord Brahma's. He performed severe austerities and finally, when the Lord appeared and was willing to offer him anything he desired, Dhruva did a volte-face—he wanted no material wealth but only God's love. Remembrance of the Lord had purified Dhruva of his lower desires and he now offered prayers immortalized in the pages of *Śrīmad-Bhāgavatam* and other scriptures. He declared that, in comparison to the Lord's personal association, which is like a priceless diamond, all the possessions and positions he had wished for in this world were like broken pieces of glass. He now only wanted the Lord's loving service.

Srila Prabhupada often said that the residents of Vrindavan are considered Krishna's best devotees because they desire nothing material from Him. They only wanted to love Him unconditionally. In one lecture, Srila Prabhupada graphically described that when Krishna returned from the pasturing grounds of Vrindavan, the gopis did not check Krishna's pockets to see what He had brought for them. They wanted nothing but His pleasure and love.

## Becoming Krishna's Dog

Srila Bhaktivinoda Thakura, a nineteenth-century Vaisnava saint from Bengal, penned many beautiful songs in his book *Sharanagati*, where, as in the following, he often echoes the mood of a devotee:

O Krishna, now that I have surrendered all I possess, kindly consider me Your dog. Chain me and maintain me, please;

I shall forever remain faithful to You. Whatever remnants
Your devotees leave after eating, I will relish them. While
sitting or lying down, I shall always meditate on Your lotus
feet. Whenever You call me, I shall run to You and dance
in rapture.[10]

Srila Prabhupada pointed out that a dog's best quality is
his loyalty to his master. Devotees sometimes compare the
neck beads they wear to a dog collar, considering themselves
Krishna's dog. We don't want to be like an uncared-for street
dog that the municipality takes away. Our neck beads may
prevent the town officials, i.e., the material energy, from
dragging us away to a world of forgetfulness of God. Krishna's
loving protection keeps us happy and safe in this world of
persistent suffering and repeated birth and death.

Following the instructions of Srila Prabhupada and our
previous acharyas, let's happily choose to be Krishna's dogs
and love and serve Him unconditionally.

# Acknowledgements

My foremost gratitude goes to His Divine Grace Srila A.C. Bhaktivedanta Swami Prabhupada, who taught by his example and teachings, the sweetness of reflective living—by slowing down our lives and remembering God naturally. This is the way to find a safe space amidst outer chaos.

My deep thanks to my spiritual master, His Holiness Radhanath Swami, who speaks from the heart, lives a fulsome, heart-centred life and serves one and all compassionately. He taught me the process of the Inner Journey.

My sincere appreciation to Govinda Prabhu, Shyamananda Prabhu, Radha Gopinath Prabhu, Sanat Kumar Prabhu, Gauranga Prabhu, Radhe Shyam Prabhu, Krishna Chandra Prabhu, Madhavananda Prabhu and Satcitananda Prabhu for their leadership and guidance to thousands of our congregation members—they help me and others find our internal Home State.

My deepest gratitude to His Holiness Bhakti Vijnana Goswami Maharaj and His Holiness Swayam Bhagavan Keshav Swami Maharaj—their lectures give me clarity and nourish me immensely.

My sincere thanks to Amarendra Prabhu, Hari Parshad Prabhu, Gauranga Darshan Prabhu and many other

ISKCON preachers whose discourses give me immense strength and happiness.

This book has seen the light of day due to the tireless management of my dear friend, Abhishek, and his wife, Hiral, who also designed the cover of the book. Shaswat and Pawan helped me with the initial proofreading and editing. My immense gratitude to Vrushnak, Disha, Mohit and Riya, for their timely feedback and help in connecting with the publishers and getting the logistical support to get this book printed. I thank my literary agent, Dipti Patel of WordFamous, for her help in connecting me with Penguin. My thanks to Gurveen Chadha, executive editor, Penguin Random House India, who showed faith in my manuscript and took it up for publication. My sincere thanks to Gunjan Ahlawat, Angelin Joy and Saba Nehal at Penguin. I also thank Shyamli Mataji, whose keen writing and reader sense helped me make important adjustments to the book.

I have learnt from many monks in our ashram as well as from various traditions. I do not take any credit for the concepts I share in this book as my realizations are derived from the healthy influences of many noble souls.

My friends in the ashram, namely, Gauranga Priya dasa, Gaur Gopal dasa, Chaitanya Charan dasa, Sikshastakama dasa, Shivram dasa, Baladeva dasa, Sri Chaitanya dasa, Manohar dasa, Nanda Dulal dasa, Mukunda Mala dasa, Radhesh Lala dasa, Vraja Chandra dasa, Prem Kishor dasa, Haridas Thakur dasa, Sudama dasa, Rudranath dasa, Rasikacharya dasa, Rasika Raman dasa, Vrajaraj Priya dasa, Anand Gopal dasa, Purushottama dasa, Nanda Gopa dasa and a hundred more have been a constant source of support and love.

My dear friends Anand Vrindavan and his wife Tulasi Mataji, and Jigar Rawal, Heet, Gautam, Jahanavi, Rajan and

Mita Padia, Palak and Paulomi Mehta, Rishab Goradia, Murari Nitai, Manasi Radhika, Dipti, Manisha, Riya, Shivam, Kumari Gopika, Jagdish, Rasa Gauranga, Aishwarya, Vaibhav Gudi, Priya Manjari, Rasa Parayana, Gopi Manjari, Jigar and Manali Shah, Nila Krishna dasa, Satyawan, Dinesh, Ramvilas, Pratik, Sameer and Manisha Thakkar, and Shifali, have contributed to help the book see the light of day.

There are many other members of the ISKCON community, both in Mumbai and all over the world, who by their constant support and encouragement helped me explore the Heart Space and share this with them. Sruti Dharma Prabhu and Prana Bandhu Prabhu's mentoring and timely guidance has shaped me in many ways. Navin Krishna, Devaki Nandan Prabhu, Kalpit Nagrecha, Vraja Raman, Braj Kripa, Vignesh Naik, Vraja Vallabh and Kadamba Kanan have been great friends in my sojourn of connection and contribution.

There are many equally dear friends and guides whom I remember daily with gratitude, but to mention all of them would make this book stretch to five hundred pages.

I sincerely thank you, the reader, for picking up this book amongst the various choices you have. I hope to please you with this small offering of service by sharing the joy of living and giving in the Heart Space.

# Notes

1  Jayant. 'Understanding the Pancha Koshas.' Science Meets Vedanta, 5 September 2020. Available at https://vedantaandscience.com/?p=639.

2  Tulchinsky, Theodore H. and Elena A. Varavikova. 'A History of Public Health'. *The New Public Health* (2014): 1–42. doi: 10.1016/B978-0-12-415766-8.00001-X.

3  Prabhupada, A.C. Bhaktivedanta Swami. *Sri Isopanishad* (The Bhaktivedanta Book Trust, 1974), purport to Mantra 3, Chapter 3. Available at https://prabhupadabooks.com/iso.

4  Harris, Russ. *The Happiness Trap* (Boulder: Trumpeter Books, 2008), pp. 9–13.

5  Serwach, Joseph. 'The Phone Is His Prison: That's Why They're Called Cell Phones', Medium, 2 December 2023. Available at https://medium.com/the-partnered-pen/the-phone-is-his-prison-thats-why-they-re-called-cell-phones-835021595937.

6  Cox, Edmund Charles. *My Thirty Years in India*. Digital Library of India, 2015. Available at archive.org/details/in.ernet.dli.2015.31023/page/n43/mode/2up.

7  Craster, Katherine. 'Contest / the Centipede's Dilemma by Mightyadd Bookmark.' *Poem Contest The Centipede's*

*Dilemma - All Poetry*. Available at https://allpoetry.com/contest/2757846-The-Centipede-s-Dilemma.

8    '20 Inspiring Slow Living Quotes.' Minimalism Made Simple, 1 March 2021. Available at https://www.minimalismmadesimple.com/home/slow-living-quotes/.

9    Prabhupada, A.C. Bhaktivedanta Swami. *Sri Caitanya Caritamrita* (Bhaktivedanta Book Trust, 1975). Available at https://prabhupadabooks.com/cc.

10   Thakur, Bhaktivinoda. 'Goptritve Varana Song 3.' *Saranagati*. Available at kksongs.org/songs/s/sarvasvatomar.html.

Scan the QR code to access the
companion audio material for this book

Scan QR code to access the
Penguin Random House India website